Arabs and Jews in Biblical Perspective

LOUIS BAHJAT HAMADA Ph.D., Litt.D.

WINEPRESS WP PUBLISHING

Printed in the United States of America

Packaged by WinePress Publishing, PO Box 428, Enumclaw, WA 98022. The views expressed or implied in this work do not necessarily reflect those of WinePress Publishing. Ultimate design, content, and editorial accuracy of this work are the responsibilities of the author.

Unless otherwise noted, Scripture quotations in this book are taken from the King James Version of the Bible.

ISBN 1-57921-245-X
Library of Congress Catalog Card Number: 99-65288

Other books by Louis Bahjat Hamada

God Loves the Arabs, Too

Understanding the Arab World

Is the Holy Land Holy?

DEDICATION

My children have prodded me to publish my life story for their perusal; and also for the benefit of those whose lives are replete with similar painful experiences. The reason I have been reluctant to do that is because I dare not expose the chronic wicked deeds of those who "thought evil against me; but God meant it unto good" (Genesis 50:20). These grueling circumstances played a meaningful role in shaping my temperament and character in order that I may be able to "bear much fruit" (John 15:8).

On the other hand, I have been tempted to write such a book, but I chose to obey my Lord and Savior, Jesus Christ, who taught me to "live peaceably with all men . . . .Be not overcome of evil, but overcome evil with good" (Romans 12:18-21)!

This is the heritage I chose to leave for my posterity: “Be ye followers of me. . . . I have fought a good fight, I have finished my course, I have kept the faith” (1 Corinthians 11:1 cf. 2 Timothy 4:7).

Contents

Foreword

THROUGH A LIFETIME of ministry, Louis Hamada's consuming passion has been to preach the gospel to all the world but especially to the sons of Ishmael, his beloved fellow Arabs. Subsidiary to this—but nonetheless important to him—has been his desire to declare that God loves all people (including the Arabs) and that he has a purpose for all the peoples, tribes, and nations of the earth. While not denying Israel's special role in the redemptive purposes of God, Hamada insists correctly that God's interests go beyond Israel, that the Lord, indeed, is nondiscriminatory in the lavish outpouring of his love and grace.

In this present work, *Arabs and Jews in Biblical Perspective*, the author does not introduce to the text of Scripture a preconceived ethnic or political agenda but lets the text itself speak concerning the important, if complicated, issue of the relationship of Jew and Arab and the plan God has for both. Utilizing his considerable literary skills, Dr. Hamada has selected a number of biblical characters and episodes that point to Arab and other non-Israelite connections to the history of salvation, painting a graphic and persuasive picture of God's loving concern for all men and women. The historical accuracy of his depictions are well documented but the narratives are not the usual dry-as-dust offerings of historiography. Rather, Hamada employs artistic imagination to "fill in the blanks" as it were, thereby producing vignettes that are delightful to read as well as spiritually and theologically edifying.

Anyone familiar with the contemporary Middle Eastern world knows how insoluble are its cultural, religious, and political tensions. Sadly, many well-meaning Christians—evangelicals in particular—take sides one way or the other, and usually on emotional or poorly conceived theological bases. There are those, on the one hand, who confuse Zionist Israel with the eschatological people of God who will, to be sure, someday embrace Jesus as Messiah but who have not yet done so. On the other hand, there are some who deny any legitimacy at all to the Jewish presence and resort to an anti-Semitism that advocates nothing short of the collapse of the Jewish state. Both positions are equally in error, and both must be soundly rejected.

As an Arab Christian, Louis Hamada has had to take a stand for truth in the midst of these thorny and contentious debates. Fully committed to the righteous cause of his own fellow Arabs, he nonetheless recognizes that God is not through with the sons of Isaac and that he is even now at work to bring to pass his eternal purposes for and through them. Embracing both believing Jews and Arabs as his brothers in Christ, he seeks in his writings and in other ways to bridge the gulf between the two and to assert that Christ is Lord of all. This book advances that objective in a delightful and compelling manner.

EUGENE H. MERRILL
Ph.D. Distinguished Professor of
Old Testament Studies
Dallas Theological Seminary

Announce to the people the pilgrimage. They will come to you on foot and on every lean camel, coming from every deep and distant highway that they may witness the benefits and recollect the name of God. (Qur'an 22:27-28)

Thy statutes have been my songs in the house of my pilgrimage. (Psalm 119:54)

One

ARABIA (YEMEN)

ARABIAN QUEEN: SEEKER OF TRUTH

STARING AT THE GRAY London sky from a small window, she wondered why she had chosen to go back now. Honors in economics, a position with British Petroleum, and the cultured life of the city—these had brought her enjoyment if not happiness. She had been away for almost twenty years; her parents had died; and only a sister and brother were there. Sensing her own uncertainty, she looked at her fellow travelers, all waiting patiently in the tiny, crowded sideroom of the mosque. Soon the clerics would come, stamp her papers, and she would be on her way. Off on a pilgrimage—who would have thought it of her? She hadn't prayed daily or consistently for years, and now she was going to Mecca. Her brother and sister, living in

Yemen, would make the trek north along the mountains and join her. She wasn't sure what to expect; she only knew the stories about white-robed men and women of every nation marching through the desert to the holy shrine. If not devoutly religious, she was at least curious. And if curiosity were not enough, she could do some business afterwards. She didn't expect to see a great light. Despite being a woman in a man's country, she would rather talk about black gold than Allah's almightiness.

Like the London lady, the Queen of Sheba[1] made an unsure pilgrimage for uncertain reasons. She went to Jerusalem, a trip of 1400 miles;[2] and considering that camels lumber along at about twenty-five miles per day, she travelled for about two months.[3] Why did Sheba leave her home to visit King Solomon? What was she seeking? Why was she all agog about the king? Was his reported wisdom simply an oddity, an amusement in which to delight?

At the time the queen visited Solomon, many scholars believe she was the pre-Islamic ruler of the southwestern Arabian country of Sheba (Saba), though some place her in northern Arabia.[4] Most do not debate her Arabic roots,[5] so the Jerusalem joust was a match of Arab and Jewish wits and wealth.

The Questioner

How did the queen hear about Solomon? Most likely from her caravaners. Solomon ruled over a country 100 by 300 miles with a population of maybe 800,000 people.[6] While the country was not huge, it was strategic; major trade routes were within its borders.

Solomon spoke some three thousand provberbs,[7] and the Queen of Sheba chose to test his wisdom with hard questions.[8] The Hebrew word for hard questions is also used for riddles or conundrums.[9] Because of the long tradition of poetry, riddles, and wise sayings among Arabic peoples the queen may have been engaging in normal court discourse.[10] It was common for the wise of the ancient Near East to visit the sages of neighboring countries and test their wisdom.[11] The Bible mentions the wisdom of such nations as Egypt, Edom, Arabia, Babylon, and Phoenicia,[12] and Solomon's fame had spread to the surrounding nations.[13]

The Queen of Sheba came from a very literate society. The Sabean language was one of the great dialects of ancient South Arabia. The script of the alphabet, with twenty-nine consonants, rivaled that of early Greek in its beauty.[14] More than ten thousand Sabean inscriptions have been found. No doubt the queen learned from the teachers and wisemen of the royal court.[15]

Numerous Judaic, Christian, Ethiopic, and Arabic traditions,[16] usually detailing three or four riddles, have suggested what the queen may have said to Solomon. One Jewish source[17] gives the following riddle:

> A woman says to her son, "Your father is my father; your grandfather is my father; you are my son and I am your sister."
>
> Solomon reportedly replied, "Surely these are the two daughters of Lot."[18]

Whether the queen initially had the curiosity of an honorable mind: that seeks the truth, it is difficult to tell. Her bantering with Solomon may have been only a diversion, a little court tomfoolery, but what had definitely drawn her and other rulers to Jerusalem was Solomon's wisdom.[19] Did God simply give Solomon wisdom on a whim, or was it a way to reveal himself to the nations and to an Arab queen? Was it another indication that God loves all nations, including Arabic ones?

The Businesswoman

Mental merriment can lead to more profound discussions, and curious questions may evoke serious answers. Perhaps the queen of Sheba examined more than Solomon's knowledge of historical trivia and asked him important questions about government and trade. Josephus indicates that Hiram, the king of Tyre, asked Solomon questions to determine if he would be a reliable ally and business partner.[20] Perhaps the queen did likewise.

Certainly the queen must have been interested in maintaining a good business relationship with Solomon. The Sabeans, as described in the first century A.D. by Pliny the Elder, were "the wealthiest race in the world because they sold that which was of the lightest weight for the highest price and bought nothing in return."[21] Pliny was probably referring to the Sabean trade in frankincense[22] and myrrh,[23] plant gum resins, the former coming from nearby lands and the latter a native product.[24] Frankincense was used in most religious offerings and myrrh for preparing bodies for burial; both had medicinal uses. Myrrh was also used as a cosmetic lotion; a six-month beauty treatment with myrrh was prescribed for Esther.[25]

The annual expenditure of Rome alone for frankincense, myrrh, and other goods from the Sabeans in the first century A.D. may have been 50,000,000 sesterces, and a sesterce was one-fourth of a day's wage. In other words, the income represented the work of about 35,000 people for everyday of a whole year. The first records of trade in frankincense and myrrh date back to the seventh century B.C., so we do not know the amount of trade income the Queen of Sheba might have received about 900 B.C.[26] We can only guess that it was significant since in addition to spices,[27] she gave Solomon 120 talents of gold,[28] a precious mineral actively mined in Arabia.[29] That was four and a half tons of gold and worth in today's money about seven million dollars.[30] Why would a smart businesswoman like the Queen of Sheba give away that much money?

One of the major Near Eastern commercial centers was Damascus, and to reach it caravans from Arabia could take the Coastal Highway or the Transjordanian Highway. Usually the trip lasted from 120-130 days.[31] The first ran along the Mediterrean coast in western Palestine;[32] the other progressed along the eastern edge of Palestine. Both international routes were controlled by Solomon, so it was essential for the South Arabians to have a trade agreement. In Roman times the taxes and expenses per camel for transporting frankincense from South Arabia to Gaza in southwest Palestine was 688 denarii, and a denarius was a day's wage.[33] Whatever the taxes in Solomon's day, the Sabean economy depended on the Damascus caravans.

Considering the wealth of Saba, why was the queen so overwhelmed by Solomon's palace, food, and servants?[34] Most of what we know about Saba comes from the seventh century B.C. or later, but much of the archaeological evidence indicates that Saba was probably quite affluent in the tenth century B.C. Only Egypt rivaled it in stone architecture; its elaborate irrigation system provided abundant food; and the queen's Jerusalem trip underscores the great number of people she had at her own command.[35]

Solomon received 666 talents of gold per year, which is roughly 25 tons or almost five and a half times the gold the queen gave to Solomon. He had two hundred large shields and three hundred small ones of hammered gold. Solomon's throne was overlaid with gold, and all his household articles and goblets were made of gold.[36]

Solomon heavily taxed the northern agricultural areas of Israel, so the abundance of food in the palace would not be surprising.[37] Just for daily life Solomon needed 560 bushels of flour and other meal, thirty head of cattle, one hundred sheep and goats, and various wild game.[38]

To maintain his household of seven hundred wives required a large staff; there were at least three hundred concubines at their service.[39] (It seems unlikely that the queen matched Solomon in husbands; in fact she may well have been a virgin queen.)[40] Whether Solomon had married all his wives at the queen's visit, we don't know; but the fact that the palace was already completed indicates that she came in at least the twenty-fourth year of his reign.[41] Because of the splendor and size of Solomon's palace and temple, many officials and servants were needed for their care.[42]

It would have been common in the tenth century B.C. to tie together a deity's blessing with human prosperity. The Queen of Sheba probably viewed Solomon's wealth as a sign of favor from his God. Because of Solomon's great wealth, she considered Solomon's God great. Solomon's wealth must have caused the queen to reflect on her own wealth and the power of her gods. David had prayed at Solomon's coronation that earthly wealth would turn people to the Owner of all things.[43] All nations needed that redirection but particularly Arab caravaners and rulers, who often made gold their god. God understood that cultural passion and Solomon's wealth may have been a tool to get Arabic peoples of the tenth century B.C. to think about the true God.

The Seeker

The queen got a peak at Solomon's mind and money, but what about Solomon's God, whose name was Yahweh? Was the queen's trip both commercial and religious?

Arabia was well-known in the centuries preceding Islam for its pilgrim fairs, a mixture of trading and tribal worship at oases.[44] Although the evidence for such fairs at the time of the Queen of Sheba is scant, they may well have existed in some form; and if so, the queen knew how to mix business and religion. At these fairs tribes declared a moratorium on fighting, brought their gods for worship, and exchanged material items. The trade in stories and poetry equaled that of goods, and talk of the supernatural was common.

Arabians typically worshipped the gods of heavenly bodies, stones, and trees.[45] The chief deities of the Sabeans were the moon god and the sun god. The title for the early Sabean rulers meant "priest-king," so the Queen of Sheba may have served as the chief priest of her faith.[46] A temple uncovered from the seventh century B.C. in Saba indicates that there were permanent worship sites.[47]

Although the Queen of Sheba probably worshipped several gods, a non-Judaic monotheism was practiced in pre-Islamic Arabia.[48] Before Islam some practiced the religion of Abraham and believed in only one God.[49] What impact monotheism had in tenth century B.C. Arabia is uncertain, but the Queen of Sheba may have been aware of the concept, either through the descendants of

Ishmael in Arabia or the offspring of Isaac in Israel. Certainly Arabic caravaners might have encountered Jewish traders and brought back reports about Yahweh to the queen.

The Queen of Sheba may have gone to Jerusalem as both religious pilgrim and philosopher, wanting to know more about Yahweh. Ancient Near Eastern wisdom embodied more than riddles and proverbs about success in everyday life. A thousand years before Solomon and the Queen of Sheba, Mesopotamians were discussing the meaning of life and the suffering of the righteous.[50] Although Solomon was well-known for his botanical and biological knowledge,[51] that was not the sum of his wisdom. He understood God's moral character and the difference between right and wrong.[52] David had prayed that his son would understand justice and righteousness and he prophesied that the rulers of Saba would bring tribute in recognition of that.[53] The coming of the Queen of Sheba to Jerusalem was a partial fulfillment of that prophecy.

If the queen and Solomon engaged in more than court repartee, what did they talk about? What did the queen ask after the temple tour? The queen may have inquired about the difference between the Arabian pantheistic gods that dwelt in trees, stones, and heavenly bodies and

Solomon's God that resided in a temple room. Drawing from his temple dedication prayer, Solomon may have told the queen that the Holy of Holies was not Yahweh's permanent dwelling place. Yahweh could not be contained in a building; not even earth or heavens could hold him.[54]

If the queen had studied genealogy and monotheism, she and Solomon may have discussed their common Abrahamic roots and their heritage through Ishmael and Isaac. Jews in the early centuries A.D. claimed that Genesis 49:10, spoken by Ishmael's half-nephew Jacob, predicted a coming eternal ruler,[55] and many New Testament writers saw references to a Messiah in the poems of Solomon's father.[56] What Solomon believed about Yahweh coming to earth in bodily form is difficult to say, but he may have pondered what Yahweh meant when he promised an eternal throne.[57] The queen proclaimed that not even half the greatness of Solomon's wisdom had been reported to her,[58] and what follows from this statement is her praise of Yahweh, which seems to imply that at least some of the wisdom Solomon imparted to her was about religious matters. After all Solomon had prayed at the dedication of the temple that foreigners would be drawn to Yahweh.[59]

The Queen of Sheba is a fascinating Old Testament character who undertook a long journey to satisfy her inquisitive mind concerning Solomon's wisdom. Her journey became proverbial and was mentioned by the Lord Jesus. What curiosity must have motivated the queen to seek the God of Solomon?

No doubt, excitement ran high as her caravan was sighted by the inhabitants of Jerusalem. The report reached the ears of King Solomon early, that a large retinue with regalia was approaching Jerusalem from the south. The dust clouds stirred by human feet and beasts of burden were so dense that the sun appeared a brilliant red. The large caravan was reported to be carrying spices: myrrh, frankincense, and many other precious goods. However, no one had ever heard of such large quantities of spices being moved at once. There would not be such excitement in Jerusalem caused by a friendly retinue until thearrival of the Magi many centuries later. Remembrance of this spice caravan from the south may have caused Solomon to write:

> Who is this coming out of the wilderness like pillars of smoke, perfumed with myrrh and frankincense, with all the merchant's fragrant powders? (Song of Solomon 3:6).

It is interesting to note that the Queen of Sheba may have been a descendant of Sheba, one of the thirteen sons of Joktan (Genesis 10:25-29). Sheba was a grandson of the patriarch Eber. His tribe colonized the area which is known today as Yemen or the Kingdom of the Sabeans. The Sabeans were greatly blessed with myrrh, frankincense, and gold. The kingdom of the Queen of Sheba was a trade route and a political center for many ancient merchant peoples. these Arab lands have produced material blessings for thousands of years. For instance, gold, frankincense and myrrh were symbols of great wealth and luxury for the mightiest civilizations. the highest tribute anyone could give to a king at that time was to offer him nature's most precious products.

Sheba and the Gifts

The generosity of the Queen of Sheba was seen in the quality and quantity of the gifts which she brought to Solomon:

> And she gave the king an hundred and twenty talents of gold, and of spices very great store, and precious stones: there came no more such abundance of spices as these which the queen of Sheba gave to king Solomon (1 Kings 10:10)

The most important gifts she gave to Solomonwere gold, frankincense, and myrrh which are immediately recognized as the three gifts that the Magi brought to Jesus at his birth in order to worship Him. The early church father Tertullian (160-230 A.D.), as well as the Arabian historian Phillip Hitti, said that the Magi were Arabs.[60] Tradition holds that Abraham gave these same kinds of gifts to his six sons through Keturah as he sent them out to the east (Genesis 25:6). Gold is used as an emblem of purity by Job. "When he hath tried me, I shall come forth as gold" (Job 23:10). It is also used to symbolize a present worthy of a king or kingly rule. In the well-known Psalm 72, it is said of Solomon (and indirectly of the Messiah), "and to him shall be given of the gold of Sheba" (Psalm 72:15).

Prophetic Implications

This amazing visit by the royalty of Sheba had been prophesied earlier. In a psalm written for Solomon, who prefigures the Messiah, it is said:

> He shall have dominion also from sea to sea,
> and from the river unto the ends of the earth.
> They that dwell in the wilderness shall bow
> before him; and his enemies shall lick the dust.

> The kings of Tarshish and of the isles shall bring presents: the kings of Sheba and Seba shall offer gifts (Psalm 72:8-10).

Of course, that greater Son of David, the Lord Jesus Christ, who has all dominion is the total fulfillment of this prophecy. The outstanding quality of spice and incense from the land of Sheba is alluded to many times after Solomon's era. Isaiah spoke of this concerning the glory of the Gentiles coming to a redeemed Zion:

> The multitude of camels shall cover thee, the dromedaries of Midian and Ephah; all they from Sheba shall come: they shall bring gold and incense; and they shall shew forth the praises of the Lord (Isaiah 6:20).

Jeremiah and Ezekiel also wrote about the spice and incense of Sheba. The Lord rebukes Israel for their turning away by the word of Jeremiah:

> To what purpose cometh there to me incense from Sheba, and the sweet cane from a far country? your burnt offerings are not acceptable, nor your sacrifices sweet unto me (Jeremiah 6:20).

The prophet Ezekiel mentions Sheba in his lamentation for the city of Tyre:

> The merchants of Sheba and Raamah, they were thy merchants: they occupied in thy fairs with chief of all spices, and with all precious stones, and gold (Ezekiel 27:22).

So the Queen of Sheba brought to Solomon the best she had in order to honor him and learn from his wisdom.

The Wisdom of Solomon

The queen was a wise woman who decided to put King Solomon to the test personally in order to verify reports of his sagacity. "She came to prove him with hard questions" (1 Kings 10:1). Tradition reports that the queen asked Solomon riddles such as:

> What is that which precedeth all, like a general; which crieth loudly and bitterly; the head of which is like a reed; which is the glory of the rich and the shame of the poor, the glory of the dead and the shame of the living: the joy of the birds and the sorrow of the fishes? Solomon answered, "Flax."[61]

How did Solomon answer so quickly? He used his expert knowledge of herbs and plants, and his knowledge of cultures to solve the riddle. Flax is evidently one of the first plants budding up in the spring; it precedes all. The wind blowing through the cultivated flax makes it sing and cry. Its head looks somewhat like a reed. Fine linen was made from it, particularly in Egypt for the clothing of the rich. Linen gloves have been found in the tomb of the Egyptian Pharaoh Tutankhamen who died in the fourteenth century B.C.[62] Coarse linen was made for the common clothing of the poor. Embalmed bodies were wrapped in linen, with the rich dead in the best linen. Men and women's undergarments were made out of linen.

Another way the Queen of Sheba attempted to test Solomon's wisdom was by dressing fair boys and sturdy girls up exactly alike so that no eye could distinguish them. The king placed water before them and bade them to wash, and then when the boys scrubbed their faces and the girls stroked theirs softly, he made out which were which.[63]

After lengthy sessions of questioning, the queen became convinced that Solomon had wisdom and discernment that surpassed "all the children of the east country, and all the wisdom of Egypt" (1Kings 4:30). Certainly after a personal interview the queen remembered the report that Solomon "was wiser than all men; than Ethan the Ezrahite, and Heman, and Chalcol, and Darda, the sons of Mahol: and his fame was in all nations round about" (1Kings 4:31).

It is not clear who Mahol was; perhaps he was not a direct progenitor of these sons, but the word *Mahol* may be simply a title.

The meaning of *Mahol* is dance or dance with joy. These wise men, therefore, may have been known as the "sons of the dance," or "the sons of joyful dancing," or possibly "the sons of song." *Mahol* is possibly the name of a musical instrument found in Psalm 150:4.

Ethan was evidently a contemporary of Solomon and the queen of Sheba. Ethan the Ezrahite wrote Psalm 89 that speaks of the covenant the Lord made with David and with his Seed who would occupy the throne of David forever (Psalm 89:28-29). Solomon was an obvious type of the Seed sitting on the throne of David, but the eternal reign of the Seed refers to the Messiah. The Old Testament doctrine of the Seed was first preached by God to the prophet Adam and his wife, Eve, (Genesis 3:15) and it was in this coming Seed that would undo the work of Satan that the Old Testament believers seemed to know about the coming Seed, or Son. For instance, an obscure Old Testament character named Agur says in a proverb:

> Who hath ascended up into heaven, or descended? who hath gathered the wind in his

> fists? who hath bound the waters in a garment? who hath established all the ends of the earth? what is his name, and what is his son's name, if thou canst tell? (Proverbs 30:4).

This phrase "ascended and descended" occurs in several places in the Old and New Testaments, and it generally has Messianic connotations.

Ethan knew about the Seed, but Solomon was wiser than Ethan. Solomon's wisdom did not consist in its height, (for many believed in the Seed), but in its breadth. Solomon understood the secret motivations of people, and he prayed that God would hear each person, "which shall know every man the plague of his own heart" (1 Kings 8:38). King Solomon had the ability to discern the incredible depravity of the human heart, and the vastness of the mercy of God. It was with this understanding that he was able to deal wisely with people.

Solomon was a wide-ranging naturalist. His knowledge of plant and animal life was used to construct proverbs to encourage other men along the path of wisdom. Solomon spoke of trees, from the cedar tree of Lebanon even to the hyssop that springs out of the wall; he spoke also of animals, of birds, of creeping things and of fish (1 Kings 4:33).

In all likelihood, the Queen of Sheba heard some of the proverbs and songs of Solomon to which we no longer have access. "And he spake three thousand proverbs: and his songs were a thousand and five" (1 Kings 4:32). It would be wonderful to know the content of these lost proverbs. For instance, the interplay between cedar and hyssop as mentioned above. The Hebrew word *ezob* is hyssop. It is a common wild plant which was used as a spice and as a cleansing brush. Hyssop was used to smear blood on the sides of the doorposts of the Hebrew houses in Egypt at the time of the Exodus. Hyssop, along with cedar woord, a live bird, and scarlet yarn was used in the purification ceremony for leprosy. Cedar and hyssop here represent the most magnificent tree and the most humble plant respectively. It is interesting to note that God planted "the cedars of Lebanon" (Psalm 104:16). Cedar symbolizes strength, splendor and longevity.[64] Hyssop represents humility, weakness and usefulness. No doubt, King Solomon pursued the richness of these themes in his proverbs.

The queen had met her match in wit and intelligence. She had met a man of compassion and wisdom in whom she could confide. Solomon was a counsellor *par excellence*; and "she communed with him of all that was in her heart" (1 Kings 10:2). Little wonder that "there was no more spirit in her" (1 Kings 10:5).

The Ethiopian Tradition

As it was mentioned before, the Ethiopian people have a tradition that King Solomon married the Queen of Sheba, and that they had a son, Menelik I. He lived in the palace in Jerusalem and became a believer in Yahweh. Menelik eventually returned to Ethiopia with other Hebrews and established the royal house of Ethiopia. The tradition relates that because of the apostasy of Israel at that time, the ark of the covenant was given by the priests to Menelik until Israel should return to the true worship of God. Again, according to Ethiopian history, the ark of the covenant rests in the deep vaults of the Church of Zion of Mary in a town named Aksum. Menelik and his returning retinue eventually became known as Falasha Jews.[65] These people still exist today in large numbers, and some of them recently immigrated to Israel to escape the military turmoil in Ethiopia.

The relationship between Sheba's country (modern Yemen) and Ethiopia is well-documented, given their trading relationships and possible early intermingling. Before the Joktanite Arabs settled the southern part of the Arabian Peninsula, there are the evidences of Cushite settlers, who appear to have passed along the south coast from west to east, and mixed with them when they arrived in the country.[66]

Menelik founded the longest-lived royal dynasty in history. The last reigning ruler was Haile Selassie who died in prison in 1975, although his heirs are still living. The royal Menelik line was interrupted in 980 A.D. by a tribal queen Gudit (Judith). She was a follower of Judaism and seemed obsessed with the idea of atacking Christianity. She attacked the royal city of Axum, leveled it to the ground, and killed the royal ruler. However, a royal prince fled to the province of Shoa in the south of Ethiopia. He married and had children which secured the survival of the royal line.[67]

Afterward, Ethiopia was ruled by Muslims beginning in the twelfth century until 1558 when the Menelik rulership was renewed. This ruling line came from Ethiopian, Arabian, and Jewish background.[68]

Ethiopia also has a venerable Christian tradition that has its beginning in the Book of Acts. Philip, the deacon, was driven by the Holy Spirit into the desert in Gaza, where he encountered a eunuch, the ruler of the treasury for Queen Candace of Ethiopia.

Philip asked the Ethiopian if he understood the passage in Isaiah which he was reading, to which the Ethiopian replied, "How can I, except some man should guide me?" (Acts 8:31). The reading in question was as follows:

> he is brought as a lamb to the slaughter, and as a sheep before her shearers is dumb, so he openeth not his mouth. He was taken from prison and from judgment: and who shall declare his generation? for he was cut off out of the land of the living (Isaiah 53:7-8).

The Ethiopian official, who was returning from worship at Jerusalem, desired to know of whom the passage in Isaiah was speaking. Philip started at Isaiah and "preached unto him Jesus" (Acts 8:35). The ruler responded, "I believe that Jesus Christ is the Son of God" (Acts 8:37). The wisdom that the Queen of Sheba heard from Solomon may well have given her an appreciation for the oral testimonies and written records about God's dealing with all peoples. Eventually these testimonies and records would become the Old Testament of which Isaiah was a part. What the Queen of Sheba may have partially understood about the Messiah, the Ethiopian was able to understand more fully with the help of Philip. This preservation of God's Word continues in the Ethiopian Coptic Church today. Philip used the apostolic method of evangelization with the Ethiopian eunuch.

The Apostolic Method

The apostolic method may be summarized in the discourse of the Lord Jesus to the two disciples on the road to Emmaus. He reproves them for their slowness of belief in his redeeming death and in his bodily resurrection.

> O fools, and slow of heart to believe all that the prophets have spoken: Ought not Christ to have suffered these things, and to enter into his glory? And beginning at Moses and all the prophets, he expounded unto them in all the scriptures the things concerning himself (Luke 24:25-27).

In this passage the Lord Jesus makes himself the supreme object of the Old Testament prophets' message, and then he shows them in various places, beginning with the Books of Moses, how he (Jesus Christ) is the key to understanding Scripture.[69] As Jesus broke bread with them, the two disciples saw him for who he was; they knew him. At that point he vanished from their sight. This must have been a very emotional experience for them, because they exclaim: "Did not our heart burn within us, while he talked with us by the way, and while he opened to us the scriptures?" (Luke 24:32).

Likewise, the Queen of Sheba's encounter with king Solomon produced similar reactions, and as she listened to the teaching of the king, "there was no more spirit in her" (1 Kings 10:5).

The Commendation of Christ

The Lord Jesus Christ himself commended the Queen of Sheba for seeking after Solomon's wisdom (Matthew 12:42; Luke 11:31). Why? The Queen of Sheba recognized that this wisdom came from someone beyond Solomon, for she said to him, "Blessed be the Lord thy God, which delighted in thee, to set thee on the throne of Israel:" (1 Kings 10:9). Jesus declared that she will condemn his generation, who lived in the light of greater spiritual revelation, for not recognizing that One greater than Solomon had come (Matthew 12:42). The Scriptures indicate that the Queen of Sheba was a believer in the God of Solomon.

Sheba in the Song

There are many theories of interpretaion of the Song of Solomon. The Song is full of metaphors, symbolism, and allegorical imagery. Some scholars interpret the Song as a picture of Israel as God's espoused bride (Hosea 2:19-20). Others believe that it is a representation of Christ's love for his Church. Although the Lord Jesus and his Church are seen in the Song, I would like to postulate briefly that the Song of Solomon seems to be written with the Queen of Sheba in mind.

As the spiritual life of a believer reaches its highest fulfillment in the love of Christ for his Church, so human love finds its highest fulfillment in the love between a man and a woman. From a human point of view the Song is a poetic record of Solomon's romantic interlude with the Shulamite.

The Queen of Sheba seems to be the most important woman in king Solomon's life, mainly because of the extensive scriptural coverage of her special relationship with Solomon. It is assumed that several verses in the Song of Solomon refer specifically to her. For instance:

> Who is this that cometh out of the wilderness like pillars of smoke, perfumed with myrrh and frankincense, with all powders of the merchants? (Song of Solomon 3:6).

Although in poetic form, this verse is probably an oblique reference to the arrival of the queen with her spice caravan.

Other verses strengthen the assumption that the queen is the Shulamite:

> I am black, but comely. O ye daughters of Jerusalem, as the tents of Kedar, as the curtains of Solomon (Song of Solomon 1:5).

The beloved is a dark-skinned beauty such as is found among the people of the Yemen (Sheba), due to Cushite and Joktanite intermarriage. Kedar is one of the twelve sons of Ishmael (Genesis 25:12-16).

Kedar means black-skinned. The tribe Kedar was comprised of skilled archers and fierce fighters. Kedar settled on the northwest part of the Arabian peninsula and the confines of Palestine (Isaiah 21:13-17). Ezekiel declares that the princes of Kedar were Arabian merchants. " . . . the princes of Kedar, they occupied with thee in lambs . . ." (Ezekiel 27:21). The people lived in black tents made of camel's hair or black goatskin. In Arabic they are called *beit sha'ar*, meaning house of hair.

The historian Philip Hitti postulates that the Shulamite woman in the Song of Solomon was the beautiful Queen of Sheba.[70] The Arabs called her *Balkis*. Solomon compares her attractive complexion with the tents of Kedar.

Solomon and his beloved spend much of their time in the song in intimate communion. Solomon calls his beloved "terrible [awe-inspiring] as an army with banners" (Song of Solomon 6:4, 10). Where would this affectionate term have come from if not from the time of their first meeting when the queen came to Jerusalem with an army of followers?

> She came to Jerusalem with a very great train, with camels that bare spices, and very much gold, and precious stones (1 Kings 10:2).

The Song is a book of intimate communion between two lovers. Scripture tells us that the Queen of Sheba "communed with him of all that was in her heart" (1 Kings 10:2). One of the best places for fellowship and communion is over an elegant meal with no time pressure to cause indigestion or hurry the conversion. This is what the beloved had, for she was "brought . . . to the banqueting house, and his banner over me [her] was love" (Song of Solomon 2:4). First Kings records that the Queen of Sheba was ushered into Solomon's banquet hall:

> And when the Queen of Sheba had seen all Solomon's wisdom, and the house that he had built, and the meat of his table . . . and his ascent by which he went up unto the house of the Lord; there was no more spirit in her (1 Kings 10:4-5).

Perhaps these events at the banquet are reflected in the Song by the phrase "Stay me with flagons, comfort me with apples: for I am sick of love" (Song of Solomon 2:5). The queen experienced lovesickness. There was no more spirit left in her, and all this occurred in the banquet house.

Is the Queen of Sheba the same as the Shulamite (Song of Solomon 6:13)? Evidently, following other biblical examples she should have been a person from Shulem. However, a place with that exact name has not been positively identified. The mystery may be solved another way. Robert Davidson in his commentary, *Ecclesiastes and The Song of Solomon*, makes the suggestion that it would be possible to give the word different pointings and it would mean "Solomon's girl."[71]

In the New Testament, Matthew,[72] writing to Jews, records Jesus' condemnation of the Pharisees for not having the seeking spirit of the Arab Queen of Sheba.[73] We do not know the depth of the queen's trust in Yahweh, but Jesus appreciated her quest, her pilgrimage, her desire for faith in something greater than herself. This Arab queen had travelled hundreds of miles to find wisdom beyond her own, and the Jewish leaders wouldn't walk next door. Luke, writing to Gentiles, gives the same story, but Jesus' words are now directed to the Jewish crowds.[74] If one Arab lady could make a sacred expedition, then Jews (and Gentile readers, including Arabs) should take the mental steps to hear the wisdom of One greater than Solomon.

The story of the queen's pilgrimage would condemn Jesus' generation in their earthly life and at their heavenly judgment; and if Jesus was doing more than just making a point, the queen will make another excursion. She will attend Judgment Day.

She will recall her search for wisdom, for enlightenment; she will reveal what Solomon told her about Yahweh. She may say that she followed the light she received. She will be overwhelmed once more as she gazes upon her fellow Arabs and most certainly her beloved Sabeans who, unlike Jesus' generation, have responded to the light of Yahweh.[75]

Pilgrimages are about finding light. Curiosity and circumstances may push a sojourner down a dark path, but only a deep, insatiable longing of the soul will keep him going through the night. For Muslims, even lapsed ones like the London lady, the journeys to Mecca, Medina, and Jerusalem are very sacred. For many the expectations are high; they want a new perception of Allah and themselves. And many will revel in Allah's almightiness,and in that respect, they will know the transcendent God of Abraham but not the personal one, the One he foresaw coming.[76] That God would be the light of the world[77] and truly explain for every seeker the words of Solomon's father —in your light we see light.[78]

That the blessing of Abraham might come on the Gentiles through Jesus Christ; that we might receive the promise of the Spirit through faith (Galatians 3:14).

Two

MOAB (JORDAN)

RUTH: A REDEEMER COMES

THE LONDON LADY, a first-time Meccan pilgrim, cautiously approached the Bedouin. She had made the trek to Mina and wanted to buy a lamb to sacrifice. The price was outrageous, but she had the money. After all she had a prestigious job with British Petroleum. She didn't like the idea of cutting the lamb's throat herself and delegated the task to another; yet she would still have to put her hand on this deputy assassin and eat some of the lamb after the slaughtering. The stench of sheeps heads and guts almost overwhelmed her, but she couldn't stop her journey now. Her life had been too empty back in London; she had to finish the pilgrimage; she had to know if that red liquid coursing from the lamb could redeem her. Was there a God who cared about her?

In the Portrayal of Ruth

A twelfth-century B.C. woman from Moab named Ruth made a pilgrimage north along the eastern side of the Dead Sea. She would ascend from more than 1000 feet below sea level to over 2000 feet above sea, turn east at the northern edge of the Dead Sea, and make her way to Bethlehem, a town six miles south of Jerusalem.[1] She would find out if Yahweh, the God of the Jews, really cared about a foreigner from the often-hated country of Moab.

It seemed unlikely that Yahweh could love a Moabitess. Moab was the incestuous fruit of Lot and his oldest daughter and the father of the Moabites.[2] He was born in the mountains near Zoar at the southern edge of the Dead Sea. Little is known about his progeny; some believe the earliest Moabites came from a "group of nomadic tribes that lived in the Syrian-Arabian desert."[3] Whatever their origin, they probably had mixed Semitic roots with the Arabic desert people being one stem.

The land of Moab extended the length of the Dead Sea on the east, though the Moabites sometimes only controlled the lower half between the Wadi Arnon and the Wadi Zered. The northern section was often a battleground and at various times became the possession of the Ammonites or other powers. Israel crossed this northern section and Moses viewed the Promised Land from Mount Nebo there. It was also here that Israel encountered the nefarious Mesopotamian soothsayer Balaam[4] and sinned with the daughters of Moab.[5] Because of this sin, 24,000 Israelites died[6] and Moabites were excluded from the assembly of God's people.

> An Ammonite or Moabite shall not enter into the congregation of the Lord; even to their tenth generation shall they not enter into the congregation of the Lord for ever: Because they met you not with bread and with water in the way, when ye came forth out of Egypt; and because they hired against thee Balaam the son of Beor of Pethor of Mesopotamia, to curse thee. Nevertheless the Lord thy God would not hearken unto Balaam; but the Lord thy God turned the curse into a blessing unto thee, because the Lord thy God loved thee (Deuteronomy 23:3-5).

The Israelites often battled Moab and were subjugated in part by their king Eglon for eighteen years.[7] Saul, David, and the kings of the divided kingdom fought with Moab. The country became a symbol of an idolatrous nation with its god Chemosh and its sacrifice of children.[8] Both Isaiah[9] and Jeremiah[10] predict future invasions and devastations for Moab.

In the context of the Old Testament, the story of Ruth is startling. Why would Yahweh be interested in a foreigner?[11] Why would Yahweh send a Jew named Boaz to rescue her and her mother-in-law from their poverty? The story of Ruth is an expression of Yahweh's love for all peoples, including those with Arabic origins.

Boaz, as a kinsman-redeemer, is an Old Testament glimpse of Jesus Christ, as the following indicates:

1. The kinsman-redeemer had to be a blood relative of Ruth through Elimelech (2:1, 3, 20); Christ is a blood relative of the human race even though He was virgin born (John 1:14; Phil. 2:7-8; Heb. 2:14).
2. The kinsman-redeemer had to have the purchase price necessary to redeem his poor brother (cf. Lev. 25:25). Boaz was a wealthy man (2:1) who was able to purchase the land that belonged to Elimelech, Naomi's deceased husband, and marry Ruth to raise up a posterity for the deceased Elimelech (4:9-10). Because Christ

was the sinless Son of God He was able to redeem a fallen human race (John 1:29; Isa. 53:5; 1 Peter 2:24).

3. The kinsman-redeemer had to be willing to redeem. Boaz was willing to buy back the forfeited property and marry Ruth (3:13; 4:9-10). Similarly, Christ willingly laid down His life to redeem the human race (Matt. 20:28; John 10:11, 17, 18; Heb. 10:9-10; 1 John 3:16).[12]

Through the marriage of Boaz and Ruth, Yahweh changed the bloodline of Israel's greatest king, David. Ruth, the non-Jew, became his great grandmother. Why would Yahweh seemingly taint the bloodline? It can only be because spiritual purity is more important to him than ethnic authenticity.

In the Prophecies of Isaiah and Jeremiah

Isaiah prophesies the destruction of the Moabites by the Assyrians in the late 700's B.C.[H13] The prophet lists fifteen Moabite cities that will wail over the coming destruction. Assyria will attack from the north and overrun northern Israel; the only refuge for Moab will be in Judah in southern Israel. The Moabites will have to escape their land at the southern end of the Dead Sea and make a getaway into the Judean Wilderness. But how can Judah show mercy to such a hated neighbor? The prophet says that such mercy can only be shown when the throne of Judah is characterized by lovingkindness, faithfulness, justice, and righteousness.[14] Perhaps Hezekiah, in part, was such an enlightened ruler, but Isaiah's words have a messianic ring.[15] Arab and Jew will never live together in peace until justice and righteousness fills the earth.

Jeremiah warns of another Moabite enemy-Babylon. This power will destroy Moab in the late 600s B.C., yet the prophet predicts that Yahweh will restore the fortunes of Moab in the latter days.[16] Perhaps this refers to some release from Babylonian captivity, but Moab never really regained its statehood after the Babylonians. The Persians followed the Babylonians, then the Greeks under Alexander the Great in 332 B.C., and the Romans in 63 B.C. Nabatean Arabs set up their capital in Petra in southern Moab, but the Romans conquered them in A.D. 106. Eventually Muslim Arabs subjugated ancient Moab in A.D. 636. Not until 1949 would the country of Jordan, modern Moab, be formed as a result of the Palestinian-Israeli conflict.

Does Yahweh have a future plan for Jordan? Isaiah and Jeremiah both seem to indicate that Jordanian Arabs will be part of Yahweh's world kingdom.

In the Birth of Jesus

Matthew traces the genealogical line of Jesus from Abraham, the spiritual father of Arabs and Jews.[17] In this lineage, he will mention four women, one being Ruth the Moabitess.[18] An all-male listing would have been customary.[19] Matthew not only mentions a woman, but one from a hated enemy—Moab. And the readers of Matthew's day would not have gained a great deal of respect for the land east of the Dead Sea, for the Nabatean Arabs rigorously controlled the Transjordanian trade routes in the first century A.D. And the Nabateans under Aretas IV assisted the Romans in taming the Jews after the death of Herod the Great.[20] Most scholars agree that Matthew wants to establish the kingly line of Jesus, but including Ruth gives Jesus a mixed ethnic heritage and hints that the Messiah would be ruler of all nations. Luke will make the point in this birth account that the baby Jesus has come as a light to the Gentiles.

> And he [Simeon] came by the Spirit into the temple: and when the parents brought in the child Jesus, to do for him after the custom of the law, then took he him up in his arms, and blessed God, and said, Lord, now lettest thou thy servant depart in peace, according to thy word: For mine eyes have seen thy salvation,

> which thou hast prepared before the face of all people; a light to lighten the Gentiles, and the glory of thy people Israel (Luke 2:27-32).

When Muslims, like the London lady, gaze on the blood of sacrificial lambs by the thousands in the Meccan pilgimage, they hope for some religious redemption. They hope the slain lamb will satisfy Allah, but this is not the price of universal salvation. Boaz redeemed a foreign girl, and Christ will take a bride from all nations with his blood. "Now therefore ye are no more strangers and foreigners, but fellow-citizens with the saints, and of the household of God" (Ephesians 2:19). Arabs and Jews are *blood* brothers, and Jordanian Arabs in the future will sing the bloodsong of the redeemed.

Then I will sprinkle clean water upon you, and ye shall be clean: from all your filthiness, and from all your idols. (Ezekiel 36:25)

Let us draw near with a true heart in full assurance of faith, having our hearts sprinkled from an evil conscience, and our bodies washed with pure water. (Hebrews 10:22)

Three

SYRIA

NAAMAN: FOLLOWER OF FAITH

SURROUNDED BY THOUSANDS, a Meccan pilgrim drank water from the Zamzam, the ancient well from which Hagar and Ishmael supposedly quenched their thirst. It was there that Allah rewarded Hagar's undying hope for herself and her son. The pilgrim also recalled the seventeenth sura (chapter) of the Qur'an in which the angel Gabriel removed Muhammad's heart, "washed the cavity with Zamzam water and filled the heart itself with faith."[1] The pilgrim had obediently followed the rites of the Meccan pilgrimage, but would this miraculous life-spring do more than heal his parched mouth? Would this ceremonial taste of water bring him renewed faith? The water was already there; he did not have to plead to Allah for it; he had only to drink it. Would this mystical imbibing cause a flood in his soul? Would he be washed clean?

Shown by the Historian's Chronicle

Like the Meccan pilgrim, an Aramean captain in Old Testament times sought physical comfort and found spiritual discomfort.[2] The Aramean, Naaman had leprosy, and he had heard through a captured Israeli servant girl that Elisha the prophet could heal him. To contact Elisha Naaman would have to journey into the land of the enemy. Naaman came from Aram, or Syria, as it came to be known in Roman times.

Aram was one of the five sons of Shem,[3] the son of Noah, and may have been the progenitor or at least the namesake, of the Arameans, though little is clear about their origin.[4] Aram was also the name of the grandson of Abraham's brother Nahor, thus the cousin of Jacob and Esau.[5] Abraham's relatives Bethuel and Laban were known as Arameans,[6] and Jacob himself was called an Aramean.[7] Some believe the Arameans were semi-nomadic peoples from the northern Arabian desert;[8] or perhaps inhabitants of the Middle Euphrates area,[9] which borders the Arabian desert on the east. Others conclude the Arameans were from the eastern Tigris region northeast of Assyria,[10] and some have decided the Arameans were not immigrants into Syria, but some of its original settlers.[11] Whatever their origin, the Arameans became a dominant force in the land north of Israel from the time of Saul to the Assyrian captivity. Their language, Aramaic, became the *lingua franca* of commercial and political life in the Middle East in the millenium before Christ and the language was spoken in Palestine by Christ and his followers.

Although the Arameans may have been Semitic relatives of the Israelites, their relationship with their southern neighbor was usually hostile, politically convenient at best. The Arameans were not even unified themselves; instead they founded small kingdom states of which Damascus became the most powerful. Like government, their religion was fragmented. They worshipped the various forms of Baal, Hadad the storm-god, Canaanite gods such as Ashtaroth, and Mesopotamian deities such as Marduk and Nebo.[12] When the military commander, Naaman, came to Israel for a miracle cure, he was entering enemy territory, both politically and religiously. This was not a family jaunt to find some long-lost Aramean cousins; he knew that Israel was the foe, a viewpoint unchanged in the Arabic Syria of today.

To placate this adversary, he brings a letter from his king and a large gift of gold, silver, and cloth rolls,[13] which may have been worth over a million dollars in today's money.[14] The king of Israel declares that he can't play God but sends Naaman and his large gift to Elisha's doorstep. Elisha does not appear but sends a messenger with the command that Naaman dip himself seven times in the Jordan river. This directive offends Naaman because his country has clear, snow-fed rivers,[15] and he probably thinks that the Jordan is nothing more than muddy backwater.

> Are not Abana and Pharpar, rivers of Damascus, better than all the waters of Israel? may I not wash in them, and be clean? So he turned and went away in a rage (2 Kings 5:12).

After some urging from his own servants, Naaman follows Elisha's orders and submerges himself seven times in the Jordan. What results from this act of faith is both physical and spiritual wholeness; Naaman has baby skin as a result of his childlike faith. He confesses monotheism.

> And he returned to the man of God, he and all his company, and came, and stood before him: and he said, Behold, now I know that there is no God in all the earth, but in Israel: now therefore, I pray thee, take a blessing of thy servant (2 Kings 5:15).

He wondered how his new faith would play back home.[16] His confession contrasts with that of most Israelites who had sought other gods under the evil reign of Jehoram.

In this Jordan bath Naaman lost both his "egocentricity and his ethnocentricity."[17] This is the story of one of the great Gentile conversion accounts in the Old Testament. It parallels that of Rahab, Ruth, and the Ninevites.[18] These Old Testament conversion stories should not be surprising because Yahweh was not the God of the Jews alone. Jews consider Abraham their father, but his relatives were called Arameans; and in a spiritual sense he is the father of all. It is neither ethnic nor spiritual confusion, for Yahweh promised that all the families of the earth would be blessed through Abraham. It was no bolt from the blue heavens forYahweh to care about Naaman, an ancestor of today's Arabic Syrians: it was the natural response of a loving, unbiased God.

Proven by the Prophet's Argument

If Elisha's miracle demonstrated that Yahweh is no respecter of persons, Amos's argument proved it. Amos wrote about the sins of the nations and the sins of Israel. Israel must have thought that they were important and that Yahweh would overlook their waywardness; they might have said they were special because God brought them up out of Egypt. Amos points out that God governs the migrations of peoples; what he did for Israel, he also did for the Ethiopians, Philistines, and Arameans.[19] Amos may have chosen the Ethiopians as an example because they were a great distance from Israel and may have been considered an insignificant region.[20] The Philistines and Arameans were neighbors but enemies. Why would Yahweh be interested in the abject or the antagonistic nations? Amos doesn't answer the question; he makes the assumption that Yahweh cares about Jews, Arabs, and all peoples.

Amos gives Israel hope by predicting that Yahweh will raise up the booth of David.

> In that day will I raise up the tabernacle of David that is fallen, and close up the breaches thereof; and I will raise up his ruins, and I will build it as in the days of old: That they may possess the remnant of Edom, and of all the heathen, which are called by my name, saith the Lord that doeth this (Amos 9:11-12).

Amos explains that this new tabernacle will include all the nations who are called by Yahweh's name. We must assume the inclusion of Yahweh-fearing Arameans, for if Yahweh chose the beginning of these ancient Syrians, he will select their end.

Explained by the Messiah's Message

The Syrians become a prototype of Yahweh's love for the nations. When Jesus settles in Capernaum in northern Israel, Matthew indicates that this fulfills Isaiah's prophecy about the Gentiles seeing a great light.[21] The good news of Jesus spread northward beyond the borders of Israel into the ancient land of the Arameans,[22] and these non-Jews came to Jesus for healing.

The ministry of the Messiah to Jews and Gentiles also fulfilled Isaiah's prophecy that this anointed One would preach good news to the poor and heal the sick.[23] Luke makes the point that Jesus' hometown of Nazareth rejected this ministry and were like Israel of Elisha's day. None of Israel's lepers in that day were healed; only the foreigner, Naaman the Syrian, had faith in the true God.[24] Luke records that the Jews on hearing Jesus' commendation of Naaman became enraged and attempted to throw him off a cliff.

> And many lepers were in Israel in the time of Eliseus the prophet; and none of them was cleansed, saving Naaman the Syrian. And all they in the synagogue, when they heard these things were filled with wrath, and rose up, and thrust him out of the city, and led him unto the brow of the hill whereon their city was built, that they might cast him down headlong. (Luke 4:27-29).

What these Jews could not understand was a Messiah that loved Gentiles, too; they did not comprehend the Abrahamic blessing to all families of the earth. They could not fathom that faith was the key, not family heritage.

Illustrated by the Apostle's Mission

That Jew of all Jews, the Apostle Paul, will find Jesus on the road to Damascus.[25] This encounter will change his view of Jews and Gentiles. At Antioch, Syria, he and Barnabas will preach to Jews and Greeks.[26] Quoting the Jewish Isaiah, Paul will declare that Christ is the light to the Gentiles;[27] and that the Jews would reject Him. The reason for this is to fulfill prophecy.

> Then Paul and Barnabas waxed bold, and said, It was necessary that the word of God should first have been spoken to you: but seeing ye put it from you, and judge yourselves unworthy of everlasting life, lo, we turn to the Gentiles (Acts 13:46).

Like the Syrian Naaman, all Gentiles should put their faith in the God above all gods, the Yahweh of the Old Testament who is the man Jesus in the New Testament and walked among Jews and Gentiles.

The historian, the prophet, and the apostle knew the heart of God. They understood that God was seeking sinners to know Him, whether Jew or Arab. "For the Son of man is come to seek and to save that which was lost" (Luke 19:10). Except for Naaman and the early Syrian Christians, most ancient Syrians did not know the God of Elisha. Assyria, Babylonia, Greece, and Rome had marched across their lands in ancient times; Turkey and France would rule them in the modern era. Between the Romans and Turks came the onslaught of Islam in 636 A.D. Islam brought the Arabic language and the faith of Muhammad into prominence. This faith would reject the God of Judaism and Christianity. Its followers, like many Jews and Christians, would choose ethnic and religious prejudice over true piety.

Their annual pilgrimage to Mecca would unite many nations. They would drink from the Zamzam, but would they find true faith? Would they find the source of living water? Its stream is deep and wide, crossing every mountain and valley, overflowing all peoples, quenching every thrist.

And they that know thy name will put their trust in thee: for thou, Lord, hast not forsaken them that seek thee. (Psalm 9:10)

Therefore it is of faith, that it might be by grace; to the end the promise might be sure to all the seed; not to that only which is of the law, but to that also which is of the faith of Abraham; who is the father of us all. (Romans 4:16)

Four

CANAAN (PALESTINE)

RAHAB: RISK TAKER FOR THE FUTURE

The Philistines

AMERICAN CHRISTIANS have managed until recently to overlook almost completely the Arab presence in the promised land. The history of the land known traditionally as Palestine bears the Arab nature of the country, until the Zionists arrived. The name Palestine was derived from "Philistia," for this was the land of the biblical Philistines, or people of the sea, who occupied the southern coastal area in the 12th century B.C. On the basis of an examination of human remains, anthropologists have discovered that the palestinians were of a racial indigenous stock of Canaanites.

Towns such as Jericho, Megiddo, and Bethshan were centers of civilization in Palestine in the early Bronze Age, and by the middle of that age, links had developed between the people in Palestine and the civilization of Phoenicia.

Throughout its long history Palestine has always been the target of successive invaders, and has rarely been free of power domination. After the Canaanites came the Egyptians and Hittites, Hebrews, Babylonians, Persians, Greeks, Ptolemies, Seleucids, Maccabees, Romans, Persians, Turks, Crusaders, Britains, and now Israelis.

During previous missionary travels to Europe, I was introduced to a converted Palestinian Muslim medical doctor living in Vienna, Austria. He had read my book, *Understanding the Arab World*, and he was interested in translating it into Arabic for the benefit of his people.

Abdallah shared with me how he had lost his profession, his property, his family, and suffered unjustly at the hands of the Israeli government. His predicament was most depressing. His housing was of the lowest quality in Vienna. His income was extremely meager, "How," I asked him, "had a professional medical man been reduced to such a deplorable situation?" Abdallah then began to recount his story.

The governmment of Israel singled out Palestinian leaders from all walks of life and used coercive methods to uproot them from their homeland. Those who refused to leave were punished. In Abdallah's case this punishment took the form of imprisonment, torture, expropriation of his property, and violation of his young wife.

His ancestral home was dynamited and his lands were confiscated. Similar stories have been advanced by many Palestinians who have been forcefully expatriated. Shortly thereafter, while imprisoned he was beaten and both arms were broken. This effectively ended his medical practice.

What Abdallah experienced seems like a repeat of Israel's first occupation of Palestine. God had told Israel to destroy the peoples of Canaan.[1] Is that God's plan—for Palestine to belong to the Jews alone? Or is God ethnically blind? Does he value the faith of all peoples? He honored the trust of the Canaanite Rahab but cursed her ancestor Canaan. In these two responses lie an understanding of how God deals with the peoples of this earth.

The Man with a Curse

Canaan, the father of the Canaanites, was one of the four sons of Ham, the son of Noah.[2] He is first remembered as the recipient of a curse, which had come because his father Ham had seen his own father Noah naked. The Bible is unclear about whether Ham engaged in some homosexual act, or other perversion. Whatever he did was an abomination to Noah.

What is more puzzling than the sin is this curse of being a "servant of servants."[3] Why on Canaan and not on Ham? Some Greek and Arabic versions of the Old Testament read "Ham" instead of "Canaan," but the latter seems the more reliable reading. One of the more clever solutions is that Noah cursed his grandson to protect himself. According to custom if he had cursed Ham, he would have brought shame on himself, but by cursing Canaan he brought shame on Ham.[4]

Not only is the reason for Canaan being cursed uncertain, but the curse itself is not clear.[5] At times the Canaanites did become servants to Israel,[6] but that was not always the case. History and archaeology simply don't reveal whether the Canaanites were more enslaved than other peoples. They were subjects of the great empires, but so also were the Jews.

Perhaps the best explanation for the curse is a general one: in some way Canaan was damned and Shem and Japheth were blessed.[7] Many understand the blessings as messianic. The Palestinian version of the Talmud sees the prophecy of blessing being fulfilled in the revelation of the Messiah.

Thus Shem was blessed with the knowledge of a saving faith in Yahweh, and Japheth was given a promise to share in that spiritual understanding.[8]

Since "the whole earth was populated" from the three sons of Noah,[9] what happens to this population reflects how God deals with humanity. And it is not being overly typological to say that cursing and blessing may denote damnation and salvation. To say it differently, all those who believe in the Lord God of Shem will receive eternal salvation, and those who reject the free gift of salvation will be damned. Ham was included among the eight persons that were saved out of the Flood: therefore, individuals from the whole human race typified by these three sons are recipients of God's saving grace. Canaan may be a type of unregenerate man; while Shem and Japheth are types of God's spiritual blessing.

Noah's three sons along with his grandson, Canaan, were used by God to show the principle behind God's curse or blessing. Some will be declared righteous by trusting God for salvation; others will be declared unrighteous through rejection of the Seed of the woman (Christ).

> And I will put enmity between thee and the woman, and between thy seed and her seed; it shall bruise thy head, and thou shalt bruise his heel (Genesis 3:15).

Luke illustrated this principle in Acts, where God demonstrated his indiscriminate love for the human race by saving one descendant from each of the three sons of Noah. The Ethiopian eunuch was a descendant of Ham;[10] Saul of Tarsus was a descendant of Shem;[11] and Cornelius was a descendant of Japheth.[12]

Noah's cursing and blessing were prophetic in nature and extended to the posterity of Canaan, Shem, and Japheth in terms of salvation and damnation. The curse on Canaan is on all those who do not believe in the Lord God of Shem for salvation. This, of course, means that descendants from all the sons of Noah will be among the saved and the damned, and some Canaanites will be saved, as the story of Rahab shows.

The Lady with the Scarlet Cord

How Rahab's forebearers arrived in Canaan is uncertain. One common view is that the Canaanites were inhabitants of Northern Arabia and migrated further north, sometime in the third millenium B.C.[13] This means that the Canaanites may have been in the Promised Land a number of centuries before Abraham and perhaps a thousand or more years before the Israelites. Although the area occupied by the Canaanites sometimes denotes the coastland of Israel, it is often the whole land west of the Jordan.[14]

> Speak unto the children of Israel, and say unto them, When ye are passed over Jordan into the land of Canaan; then ye shall drive out all the inhabitants of the land from before you, and destroy all their pictures, and destroy all their molten images, and quite pluck down all their high places: (Numbers 33:51-52).

There were a number of peoples who shared this land with the Canaanites such as the Hittites, Hivites, Girgashites, and Jebusites, but the most prominent group was the Amorites. Sometimes the terms *Canaanite* and *Amorite* seem interchangeable,[15] but they are different peoples. The Amorites settled in the hill country and the Canaanites in the plains.[16] The Amorites may have originally invaded Jericho, but by the time of Rahab the Canaanites had probably lived in Jericho for centuries.[17]

Jericho was a small oasis village and probably would have been ignored by the Israelites except for its location near the Jordan River. It was a gateway from the east into Canaan, so it was natural for the two spies to survey the city.[18] What Rahab reveals to the two spies of her knowledge of Yahweh is startling. She knows what he has done in the past—dried up the Red Sea;[19] what he has done in the present—defeated the two kings of the Amorites, Sihon and Og;[20] and what he will do in the future—give Israel the land. She truly believes that Yahweh is the God of heaven and earth.[21]

The Canaanites were polytheistic and sacrificed to various gods. Their chief god was Baal, the god of rain, and Rahab must have known that Jordan was overflowing its banks with water at the time the spies came.[22] Yet she proclaims that Yahweh is a God who can change the course of a sea.

The Canaanites were not backward people; they were exceptional engineers, creative artisans, enterprising merchants, and ingenious inventors.[23] They had developed a city-state form of government with a king at the head.[24] Rahab may have been an uneducated prostitute, but she was as savvy as her culture. Yet she puts all she has known aside to embrace this Yahweh of the Israelites. This willingness to risk all made her one of the great women of faith.[25]

Rahab marks her house with a scarlet cord so that the invading troops of Israel will not kill her and her family. That cord is a tangible sign of her faith; she truly believed that the spies would keep their word and that Yahweh was more powerful than any of her gods. Her salvation shows that God had not cursed all the Canaanites; he loves both Arabs and Jews. Why did God destroy the rest of Jericho? The writer of Hebrews says it was because of disobedience.[26] Yahweh had told Israel to destroy the Canaanites because of their wickedness as shown in their sacrificing of children.[27]

After the destruction of Jericho, Rahab and her family lived with Israel.[28] She married a Jewish fellow named Salmon and had a son named Boaz.[29] Boaz, half-Arab and half-Jew, takes an Arab wife, Ruth. Their grandson Jesse is the father of King David. Israel's greatest king is not a pure Jew, but through his lineage the Messiah will come.[30]

James will use Abraham and Rahab as his two great examples of working faith.

> Was not Abraham our father justified by works, when he had offered Isaac his son upon the altar? Seest thou how faith wrought with his works, and by works was faith made perfect? And the scripture was fulfilled which saith, Abraham believed God, and it was imputed unto him for righteousness: and he was called the Friend of God. Ye see then how that by works a man is justified, and not by faith only. Likewise also was not Rahab the harlot justified by works, when she had received messengers, and had sent them out another way? For

> as the body without the spirit is dead, so faith without works is dead also (James 2:21-26).

It is a divine pairing, for both demonstrate that faith has no ethnic bounds. Abraham may be the father of the Jewish nation, but he was not a Jew; he was Mesopotamian. He was also the father of many nations, including the eighteen Arabian nations through Hagar and Keturah.[31] Rahab, the Canaanite and ancestral mother of Jesus, probably has a northern Arabian heritage.

Both Abraham and Rahab believe God, and that is all that counts.

The People without a Country

If God valued the faith of the non-Jews Abraham and Rahab, why are Christian Palestinians like Abdallah without a country? The current Middle East turmoil results from an ignorance of precisely what the Bible has promised, and to whom the land was divinely ordained. With the continued expansion of Israel, the question must be raised as to whether the Jews have an exclusive divine right to the Promised Land, or was this right the result of political pressure and military conquest.

When God said to Abraham that he was going to give the land to his descendants as "an everlasting possession,"[32] more than Jews must be included in the promise. The promise was made before the birth of Ishmael and before the birth of Isaac. The only time the land was under an exclusively Jewish control was during the period of King Solomon's rule.[33] The Palestinians and other Arabs have always lived side by side with the Jews in the Promised Land.

God put the Jews in Palestine to be a light to the nations that had forgotten him; he could have placed them anywhere on earth. God was more interested in their testimony than in *terra firma*. Nevertheless, history must have a stage, and God chose a crossroads land of the ancient world to reveal himself. The choice had more to do with strategy than sacredness. Palestine served as the birthplace and deathplace of Jesus,[34] and it will be the restingplace of history.[35] Palestine is special because of what Jesus has done and will do there, but the dirt is not divine. Only God is holy, not the land. The Promised Land has been appointed unto destruction along with the whole earth, since the time of Adam.[36] It is under the curse of God until its final destruction, when its "elements will melt with fervent heat."[37] It will become holy when the holy city descends from heaven.[38]

Noah's curse on Canaan is not directly related to any particular segment of the human race, and any such view is man's way of justifying his own pride and prejudice. The deep-rooted racial problems between Arabs and Jews, and between other groups, might be alleviated if the faith of Rahab was better understood. Her faith, though not complete, looked forward to a time when God would rescue all peoples.

While the earth remains under the curse of God,[39] Christ's death abolished the curse on Canaan and his descendants. Anyone who comes to God through faith in Christ the Savior, irrespective of nationality, partakes in the Abrahamic blessing,

> for [we] are all sons of God through faith in Christ Jesus . . . And if [we] are Christ's then [we] are Abraham's seed, and heirs according to the promise.[40]

The only persons who are still under the curse of God are those, like the inhabitants of Jericho, who failed to exercise faith. The faith of Rahab is the true hope of Jews and Arabs. It is the faith for all ages and peoples.

There is joy in the presence of the angels of God over one sinner that repenteth. (Luke 15:10)

When they heard these things, they held their peace, and glorified God, saying, Then hath God also to the Gentiles granted repentance unto life. (Acts 11:18)

Five

Assyria (Iraq)

Ninevites: Repenters of the Past

Like ancient Assyria, modern Iraq has been known for its military might; yet all has not gone well in recent years. From 1980 through 1988 they waged a war with Iran, which they lost. In 1990 they invaded Kuwait and were convincingly overpowered by the United States in its Desert Storm campaign. In October 1994 they again put troops near the Kuwaiti border, only to be rebuffed by America and the United Nations. A year before this last troop movement three Christians journeyed to Iraq to assess the political and spiritual situation; they wanted to pray intelligently for this torn nation. These three crossed at the Turkey-Iraq border without incident. Although they encountered fighting in some areas, they were able to question Iraquis about their lives. "The Iraqi people were friendly but lacked hope for their lives and futures. An individual who regularly takes Bibles into Iraq told the prayer team that Iraquis were disillusioned since the Gulf War. Many Iraquis believed something must be wrong with their religion since their god was unable to help them win the war."[1]

The three found that Islamic belief and governmental oppression were the two main causes of disouragement, but that the people were "more open to the gospel than people in many other Muslim nations."[2] Since returning from their journey, the three have been praying that "Muslims will be disillusioned with Allah who was unable to save them from the destruction of the Gulf War, that they will have the veil of deception removed, and that they will come to know Jesus Christ."[3] It is almost a prayer that Jonah could have prayed, but he wanted nothing to do with ancient Iraq. In his eyes Assyria was a fearsome and wicked nation.

Assyria is the first great empire after the Flood. The Bible traces the origins of Assyria to Nimrod, the grandson of Ham, one of the three sons of Noah.[4] He founded several Assyrian cities, including Nineveh. Another root comes from Ham's brother Shem, the father of Asshur, who supposedly migrated to Assyria.[5] Except for these brief citations from the Table of Nations in Genesis, the history of Assyria is uncertain.

Ancient Assyria occupied what is today the northern section of modern Iraq; Babylon was in the south, and both drew their subsistence from the fertile plains of the Tigris and Euphrates rivers. The early settlers of Assyria were probably wandering tribes; after that came agricultural settlements in the Hassuna plains. What followed was the Halaf culture, probably from northern Assyria, that emphasized village life and commerce. Developing in southern Mesopotamia were the Ubaid peoples, who spread north as they traded in timber and copper. By the fourth millennium B.C. the Sumerians became a force in southern Mesopotamia, building large temples and powerful city-states. About this time, the Akkedians, a Semitic-speaking group form the western Syrian desert, settled north of Sumeria. One of their leaders, Sargon (2371-2316 B.C.), conquered southern Mesopotamia and the northern area we know as Assyria, controlling Nineveh. What is evident from these early times is that the Assyrians were probably an ethnic mixture with a Semitic language, related to both the later languages of Hebrew and Arabic.[6] Part of that ethnic mixture was probably Arabic coming from the

Syro-Arabian desert.[7] Today 80 percent of Iraq's inhabitants are Arabs, and Arabic is the official language as a result of the Muslim invasions of the seventh century A.D.

Much of what the Bible has to say about Assyria occurs after the split of Israel's kingdom into two kingdoms in 931 B.C. At this time Assyria had established a powerful political dynasty and its military might was dominant. Assyria is a constant nemesis to both kingdoms but particularly the northern kingdom. Tiglath-pileser III (745-742 B.C.) will harrass the northern kings Menahem (752-742 B.C.)[8] and Pekah (752-732 B.C.)[9] and the southern king Ahaz (735-715 B.C.).[10] The next Assyrian king Shalmaneser V (727-722 B.C.) will overrun Hoshea (732-722 B.C.) and the northern kingdom.[11] Sargon III (721-705 B.C.) will complete the task, and Sennacherib (704-681 B.C.) will continue to apply pressure to Hezekiah (715-686 B.C.) and his southern kingdom of Judah.[12]

From the histories in the Kings and Chronicles and the pronouncements in the prophets,[13] Assyria appears to be one of Israel's all-time enemies. Assyria's kings will describe themselves as "merciless, despots of all lands, mighty heroes clothed in terror, consuming and unquenchable fires, the terrible hurricanes."[14] They will talk of the "heavy yoke of rule, the unsparing weapon that utterly destroys the enemy's land, and the filling of the plains with blood."[15] On the memorial stele of one king are the words: "Three thousand captives I burned with fire. I left not one hostage alive. I cut off the hands and feet of some. I cut off the noses, ears, and fingers of others. The eyes of numerous soldiers I put out. Maidens I burned as a holocaust."[16] How could Israel or its God love such a people?

The Assyrians also worshipped other gods; in fact every city probably had a god. Ashur was the great lord, the father of gods, but Marduk, Nabu, and Ishtar were just some of the other gods.[17] Of one god it is said, "He wears the heavens on his head like a turban; he is shod with the underworld as with sandals."[18] To these gods the Assyrians built temples, or ziggurats. These places of worship were as big as two-hundred feet square with up to seven levels.[19] There they made meat offerings and evoked the blessings of the gods. The Assyrians not only had blood on their hands but also sacrilege on their lips, and yet Yahweh loved them.

Yahweh's love for these ancient Iraqis seems inexplicable if the Old Testament is nothing more than a testimony of Yahweh's singular devotion to the Jews. When Yahweh repeated the Abrahamic promise to Jacob, he proclaimed that his descendants would spread in all directions, including east, and that blessing would come to all of earth's families.[20] Yahweh promised Jacob, the man with the Aramean wives, this blessing centuries before the Jewish nation was formed in the womb of Egypt. One nation that developed directly east of Jacob's homeland was Assyria, and these peoples of mixed ethnic origins were not Jews. In Old Testament terms, they were heathens, Gentiles. What changes our understanding of these peoples is the story of Jonah.

The Man from Gath-hepher

Outside of the book bearing his name, Jonah, from the Galilean town of Gath-hepher, is only mentioned in 2 Kings 14:28, where he prophesies the restoration of Israel to Davidic borders by Jeroboam II (793-753 B.C.). Jonah has been greatly revered by Christianity, Judaism, and Islam. He is the only major or minor Old Testament prophet mentioned in the Qu'ran, and the Qu'ran presents an abbreviated version of the Jonah story.[21] The Qu'ran applauds the people of Nineveh for their faith.[22] The response of the Ninevites and Yahweh, however, angers Jonah.

Jonah does not want to preach to the people of Nineveh. If the events of Jonah took place in the first half of the eighth century B.C., Assyria was in a temporary period of decline, but her might was still widely known. Jonah probably wanted Yahweh to simply judge this wicked people; there was no need for him to make a month-long trek of 500-plus miles on donkeys or camel to Nineveh.[23] These people were not evil Jews but degraded Gentiles. They were uncircumcised; they followed after many gods. Why would Yahweh want them in his kingdom?

When Jonah finally makes it to Nineveh after his boat and fish rides, he marches through the city for three days, giving one of the shortest sermons on record, "Yet forty days, and Nineveh shall be overthrown."[24] He doesn't tell them to repent because he is probably still mad at Yahweh and hopes the Assyrians will meet their doom. The Assyrians may have been psychologically ready for Jonah's message. A serious plague had swept over the city in 765 B.C., and on June 15, 763 B.C., a total solar eclipse darkened the land. Another plague occurred in 759 B.C.[25] If there had been some omen of evil before Jonah came, the Assyrians may have been checking out Jonah's message as they would have any diviner or wiseman. Nevertheless, the response is dramatic; the king orders fasting and sackcloth for both humans and animals.[26] The Assyrians are to call on Yahweh and turn from their wicked ways.[27]

Yahweh sees true repentance and decides not to punish them.[28] What had been their intended punishment is unclear; but this stay of execution is ironical, for only a few decades after this the Assyrians will ravish northern Israel.

What does seem to be clear is that Yahweh indiscriminately shows mercy to repenting individuals, including non-Jews, regardless of his overall plans.

Yahweh's mercy results in Jonah's anger, and Yahweh will use a plant, a worm, and an east wind to teach Jonah about compassion.[29] Jonah is upset because his shade plant is killed by a worm and he is scorched by a hot wind. Yahweh points out that Jonah has more compassion for the plant than he does for the 120,000 people in Nineveh, who "deserve compassion not only as creatures for whom God cares but also as virtual children compared with the Jews."[30] Jonah had wrapped himself in "smug prejudice and exclusinve solidarity," forgetting that the wideness of God's mercy cannot be measured.[31] "No one is excluded from the salvation purposes of God for his creation. Israel has no claim on God's salvation that would enable her to set anyone else outside, even the most wicked among the peoples of the world."[32]

The Sign of Jonah

While Israel had no exclusinve claim on God's salvation, her knowledge of God's ways should have brought devotion instead of degradation. Jesus will point out to the Jews of his day that the Ninevites understood the sign of Jonah.[33] We have no record in the Book of Jonah that the prophet told the Ninevites about his dip in the deep, but the words of Jesus imply that the Ninevites may have known about the miracle. If so, the Ninevites readily accepted the power of Yahweh to control nature. Because many of the Assyrian gods were involved with nature, belief in the fish story may not have been a great leap of faith, but it was faith nonetheless-more faith than the Jews of Jonah or Jesus' day could muster. These ancestors of the Arabic Iraqis are exhibiting a faith that Jews will not claim. As a type, Jonah pictured the death and resurrection of Christ. First-century Jews could not believe that Christ had power over death; if he had demonstrated that power, he would have been God.

On the day of Pentecost Peter will reiterate the sign of Jonah when he claims that Christ was not abandoned to Hades, or the grave.[34] Jews from Mesopotamia[35] will hear this message and presumably some will believe. They will take the message east from Jerusalem and they might well have shared it with some of their Gentile neighbors in the land that was once called Assyria. Although most of the more than 22.4 million people living in Iraq today are Muslims, there are approximately one million Protestant Christians living in Iraq today. Some of whom are descendants of believers in the first century after Christ.

The Word of Isaiah

Although Assyrians turned to Yahweh in Jonah's day and confessed Christ in the early centuries after the Resurrection, they will become a national blessing at the close of history. What's surprising about this is that many Bible students see only Israel as God's special nation; moreover, Assyria hardly qualifies as a stalwart of godly principles in the Old Testament. In Isaiah 9-10 the prophet describes three governments: the just one of the Prince of Peace,[36] the corrupt one of Israel,[37] and the avenging one of Assyria.[38] Because Israel will not embrace Yahweh's just government, they will face the unjust government of Assyria. Although Assyria will carry out Yahweh's justice, they will also be subservient to it, for Yahweh will crush and trample them.[39] What is clear from Isaiah is that all nations, both Jew and Gentile ones, have failed to live up to Yahweh's standard of justice. Despite this, Yahweh will display his grace toward all nations, and particularly toward Assyria. In the last days he will make Assyria a blessing on the earth and will call her the work of his hands.[40] She will worship him.[41]

The time-bound response of the Assyrians in Jonah's day is replaced by an eternal one from the Assyrians at the close of time. She will join Egypt and Israel in their worship and be considered an equal partner in sharing God's blessing with the rest of the earth. That God would create this unlikely triumvirate of two Arab nations and a Jewish one can only indicate his love for all of humanity. Assyria may have stayed Yahweh's hand in Jonah's day through repentance, but her future glory will be guaranteed by God's grace and love alone.

For God is my King from of old, working salvation in the midst of the earth. (Psalm 74:12)

By me kings reign, and princes decree justice. (Proverbs 8:15)

So shall He sprinkle many nations; the kings shall shut their mouths at him: for that which had not been told them shall they see; and that which they had not heard shall they consider. (Isaiah 52:15)

Six

PERSIA (IRAN)

PERSIAN KINGS: SERVANTS OF A HIGHER GOD

A CERTAIN KING believed that what he had been taught, and what he believed, was right. In many ways he was a just man, but he was one whose ideas were limited.

One day he said to his three daughters:

"All that I have is yours, or will be yours. Through me you obtained your life. It is my will which determines your future, and hence determines your fate."

Dutifully, and quite persuaded of the truth of this, two of the girls agreed.

The third daughter, however, said:

"Although my position demands that I be obedient to the laws, I cannot believe that my fate must always be determined by your opinions."

"We shall see about that," said the king.

He ordered her to be imprisoned in a small cell, where she languished for years. Meanwhile the king and his obedient daughters spent freely of the wealth which would otherwise have been expended upon her.

The king said to himself:

"This girl lies in prison not by her own will, but by mine. This proves sufficiently for any logical mind, that it is *my* will, not hers, which is determining her fate."

The people of the country, hearing of their princess's situation, said to one another:

"She must have done or said something very wrong for a monarch, with whom we find no fault, to treat his own flesh and blood so." For they had not arrived at the point where they felt the need to dispute the king's assumption of rightness in everything.

From time to time the king visited the girl. Although she was pale and weakened from her imprisonment, she refused to change her attitude.

Finally the king's patience came to an end.

"Your continued defiance," he said to her, "will only annoy me further, and seem to weaken my rights, if you stay within my realms. I could kill you; but I am merciful. I therefore banish you into the wilderness adjoining my territory. This is a wilderness, inhabited only by wild beasts and such eccentric outcasts who cannot survive in our rational society. There you will soon discover whether you can have an existence apart from that of your family; and, if you can, whether you prefer it to ours."

His decree was at once obeyed, and she was conveyed to the borders of the kingdom. The princess found herself set loose in a wild land which bore little resemblance to the sheltered surroundings of her upbringing. But she soon learned that a cave would serve for a house, that nuts and fruit came from trees as well as from golden plates, that warmth came from the sun. This wilderness had a climate and a way of existing of its own.

After some time she had so ordered her life that she had water from springs, vegetables from the earth, fire from a smoldering tree.

"Here," she said to herself, "is a life whose elements belong together, form a completeness, yet neither individually nor collectively do they obey the commands of my father the king."

One day a lost traveler—as it happened a man of great riches and ingenuity—came upon the exiled princess, fell in love with her, and took her back to his own country, where they were married.

After a space of time, the two decided to return to the wilderness where they built a huge and prosperous city where their wisdom, resources and faith were expressed to their fullest possible extent. The "eccentrics" and other outcasts, many of them thought to be madmen, harmonized completely and usefully with this manysided life.

The city and its surrounding countryside became renowned throughout the entire world. It was not long before its power and beauty far outshone that of the realm of the princess's father.

By the unanimous choice of the inhabitants, the princess and her husband were elected to the joint monarchy of this new and ideal kingdom.

At length the king decided to visit the strange and mysterious place which had sprung up in a wilderness, and which was, he heard, peopled at least in part by those whom he and his life despised.

As, with bowed head, he slowly approached the foot of the throne upon which the young couple sat and raised his eyes to meet those whose repute of justice, prosperity and understanding far exceeded his own, he was able to catch the murmured words of his daughter:

"You see, Father, every man and woman has his own fate and his own choice."[1]

Supposedly the great Muslim teacher, Ahmed el-Rifal, told this story to the Sultan Saladin, in response to a question about what part the decrees of rulers play in the welfare of their people. At first the tale seems to glorify individual choice; but there is another level to the story, for the commands of the father force the choices of the daughter. And who controls the dictates of the king? Is there someone behind both kings and their subjects? Are the fates and choices of both potentates and their peoples more than chance? The stories of four Persian kings in the Bible help us understand who is the real King and who are the servants. To appreciate these four vignettes we must go back to the dawn of history.

The table of nations in Genesis 10 gives us the origin of two geographical areas in Persia, or ancient Iran. One of the sons of Shem was Elam, the father of the Elamites, a people who populated the southwestern section of the land, known today as Khuzestan.[2] One Elamite king in the Bible was Chedorlaomer, who captured Lot but lost a battle with Abraham.[3] In the second millennium B.C. the Elamites were a dominant political force, capturing Babylon around 1175 B.C. and taking Hammurabi's law code as a spoil.[4] The

Assyrians and the Persians eventually overran the small empire.[5]

A son of Japheth was Madai, the probable progenitor of the inhabitants known as Medes in northwestern Iran around the Caspian Sea.[6] Historians consider them non-Semitic, indicating that some of the descendants of Noah's three sons migrated from the Middle East, formed people groups, and then returned in later migrations. Whatever the origins of the Medes, the main migrations of peoples into Iran seemed to have come about 1500 B.C. from the Austro-Hungarian plains or from southwest Russia.[7] These people were known as Aryans, or Indo-Europeans.

What has given all the peoples of Iran an Arabic connection has been the influence of Islam. Although Iranians speak Persian (Farsi), much of the legal, political, philosophical, and religious vocabulary is Arabic, and the language is written in Arabic script. About 90 percent of Iranians belong to the Shi'a branch of Islam; the rest are Sunnis.[8]

The Anointed Shepherd

The Second Book of Chronicles ends its history of Israel with the declaration that Cyrus, king of Persia, will decree the return of the Jews from Babylon to their homeland.[9]

> Thus saith Cyrus king of Persia, All the kingdoms of the earth hath the Lord God of heaven given me; and he hath charged me to build him an house in Jerusalem, which is in Judah. Who is there among you of all his people? The Lord his God be with him, and let him go up (2 Chronicles 36:23).

This decree fulfilled the words of Jeremiah[10] and was caused by God stirring up the spirit of Cyrus.[11] What the chronicler records in two verses, Isaiah explains in two chapters.[12] Isaiah described Yahweh as Creator,[13] King,[14] and Redeemer,[15] the one who will pour out his Spirit and blessing on Israel's descendants. This blessing recalls the Abrahamic Covenant in which Yahweh promised to bless all the families of the earth through Abraham's Seed.[16] Yahweh will fulfill his promises in part to Israel by bringing them back from their captivity in Babylon, but he will do it in an unexpected way. He will use the Gentile king, Cyrus the Great, to be the shepherd of Israel.[17] What seems particularly glorious is that Yahweh will reveal himself to a Persian king, showing again his regard for all peoples. That does not happen by accident. In fact Isaiah indicates that Cyrus, though he is called Yahweh's anointed,[18] does not know Yahweh.

> Thus saith the Lord to his anointed, to Cyrus, whose right hand I have holden, to subdue nations before him; and I will loose the loins of kings, to open before him the two leaved gates; and the gates shall not be shut; I will go before thee, and make the crooked places straight: I will break in pieces the gates of brass, and cut in sunder the bars of iron: And I will give thee the treasures of darkness, and hidden riches of secret places, that thou mayest know that I, the Lord, which call thee by thy name, am the God of Israel. For Jacob my servant's sake and Israel mine elect, I have even called thee by thy name: I have surnamed thee, though thou hast not known me. I AM the Lord, and there is none else, there is no God beside me: I girded thee, though thou hast not known me: (Isaiah 45:1-5).

Although Cyrus was chosen by God to accomplish his good purpose for Israel, he received no spiritual reward for his good work.

> I have raised him [Cyrus] up in righteousness, and I will direct all his ways: he shall build my city, and he shall let go my captives, not for price nor reward, saith the Lord of hosts (Isaiah 45:13).

This seems strange; after all Cyrus was one of the more enlightened kings of antiquity. He respected local customs and was tolerant of other religions. Why doesn't Yahweh reveal himself to this good king? Whereas Isaiah gives no answer, the Lord Jesus clarifies this spiritual mystery in John 2:23-25:

> Now when he was in Jerusalem at the passover, in the feast day, many believed in his name, when they saw the miracles which he did. But Jesus did not commit himself unto them, becasue he knew all men, and needed not that any should testify of man: for he knew what was in man.

Moreover, Isaiah does not portray Yahweh as a God of the Jews alone. Yahweh is a God who will save "all the ends of the earth."[19] Although the actions of Cyrus may not have spiritually benefitted him, they will eventually bring spiritual gain to his progeny. If viewed from the perspective of a timeless God, Cyrus's endeavors directly link him with the Arabic-influenced, Islamic Iranians of today.

The Lion King

At seventy years of age Cyrus launched a military campaign in northeastern Persia. Shortly thereafter in July of 530 B.C. he was killed in a battle; his tomb reportedly had this inscription:

> Mortal! I am Cyrus, son of Cambyses, who founded the Persian Empire, and was Lord of Asia. Grudge me not, then, my monument.[20]

Cyrus was succeeded to the throne by his son, Cambyses II, who ruled a short time and then committed suicide in Syria in 522 B.C.[21] Darius, a member of the royal family, gained control in 521 B.C. by putting down a series of revolts. He made Susa, the old Elamite capital, the administrative capital, and he created a coinage system of gold and silver. He reorganized the empire and divided it into provinces, or satrapies. However, this Darius was Achaemenian and not a Mede, like the Darius of Daniel.[22] Daniel's Darius has been identified as Cyrus, Gubaru I, the conqueror of Babylon, and Gubaru II, the governor of Babylon.[23] The term *Darius* may have been a title of honor like that of "Caesar" in Rome.[24]

Whatever his identification, this Darius of Daniel appointed 120 satraps, or provincial governors over the newly conquered Babylon.[25] Over these governors were three commissioners, of whom Daniel was one.[26] Because of Daniel's administrative gifts, Darius considered placing

Daniel over his entire kingdom;[27] which caused the other officials to be jealous and to seek a way to remove Daniel from office. They petition Darius to make an injunction against worshipping anyone besides the king, thus trapping Daniel and orchestrating his imprisonment with the lions.[28] When Daniel is delivered from the lions, Darius publicly proclaims that all citizens are to honor Yahweh. His statements about Yahweh seem to reveal a deeper understanding than that of Isaiah's Cyrus. Darius declares three things about Yahweh:

> (1) [He] is alive and shows that he lives by the way he acts in history, responding, like a real person, to the requirements of justice and the needs of his people;
>
> (2) [His] rule is eternal and will never pass away (as do empires built by human power), even though the Hebrew monarchy did not survive its apostasy;
>
> (3) [He] miraculously delivers his true worshippers, performing wonders both in heaven and on earth. He has furnished objective proof of his eternal power and godhead, in contrast with all other deities.[29]

Whatever the level of Darius's belief, his proclamation was bound to have affected thousands of people, for it was sent throughout the Persian empire and in every language of the empire. And in a personal way the peoples of the Zagros Mountains and the province of Gutuim may have taken note, for that may have been the home of Darius.[30] Except for the Jews of the Captivity and some still in Israel, those who heard this declaration would have been Gentiles, mostly Aryans but also Elamites and Arabs in the south. Yahweh was spreading his message to all peoples.

The Merciful Kings

The book of Ezra chronicles the rebuilding of the temple, and evidently the original decree of Cyrus had been lost. The Jews petition Darius I to search for the decree so that work on the temple may continue.[31] Darius I does a search and locates the document in Ecbatana, Persia.[32] He reissues the decree and adds some commands of his own.[33] There is no indication that this Darius has the same revelation about God as Darius the Mede, but the preserving of worship in Israel continues Yahweh's plan of blessing all nations.

The story of Esther introduces Ahasuerus, or Xerxes, the son of Darius I. Xerxes is ruling from Susa in southwestern Persia. The tale of Esther and its court intrigue are well-known. Esther saves her people, Haman is hanged, and Mordecai is honored. It is a story of Jews who decided to stay in the land of the enemy rather than return to the homeland. The drama unfolds in Gentile territory. Strikingly, the book of Esther never mentions the word *God,* although his providence is definitely implied.[34] Jews still celebrate that providence in the annual Feast of Purim. Although Xerxes is more in the mold of Cyrus than Darius the Mede, his part in Yahweh's plan to preserve the Jews is without debate. What is not often mentioned is that he preserved his own people as well, thus securing again the Gentile blessing of the Abrahamic covenant; which is: " . . . and in thee shall all families of the earth be blessed:" (Genesis 12:3).

The King of Kings

On the Day of Pentecost Peter preached that God would pour out his Spirit on all mankind.[35] Luke lists peoples from sixteen nations who heard Peter's message. Three of these peoples were Parthians, Medes, and Elamites, probably diaspora Jews from the east, north, and south of what was once ancient Persia. Peter had proclaimed that Jesus was the Messiah, the anointed One, a forgiver of sins and a sender of the Holy Spirit.[36] The promise of forgiveness and God's Spirit was not only for Jews but for "all who are afar off."[37] Assuming that some of these Jews from Parthia, Media, and Elymais were among the three thousand converts, the gospel made its way rather quickly into what is now Iran and probably among some Gentiles.

The predominant religion there in first century A.D. may have been Zoroastrianism, founded by the prophet Zoroaster, who followed Ahuramasda, "the wise lord."[38] It is uncertain whether Zoroastrianism was monotheistic or henotheistic (one god above other gods). Adherents were urged to choose between two opposing principles, righteousness and the lie.[39] But Jesus offered more than righteousness; he brought forgiveness. Zoroaster preached that salvation depended on works alone and that man would be judged by weighing good deeds against bad deeds.[40] We can only guess at how widespread this forgiveness of Jesus might have been preached in Iran in those early years after Pentecost. What is certain is that God continued to reach out to the Gentiles, and in this case, to the ancestors of twentieth-century, Islam-dominated Iranians.

Homer, the Greek, writhing almost two centuries before Cyrus, says in his *Iliad*, "A multitude of rulers is not a good thing. Let there be one ruler, one king." The Psalmist exclaims, "Who is this King of glory? The Lord of hosts, he is the King of glory."[41] He will rule in the hearts of kings and subjects to bring salvation to many.

NOTES

Chapter One

1 Sheba was a descendant of Cush, son of Ham (Gen 10:7); a son of Joktan, a descendant of Shem (Gen 10:28); or the oldest son of Jokshan, a child of Abraham by Keturah (Gen 25:3). It is unclear whether these instances of the name Sheba refer to one, two, or three persons. It does seem likely that the country in southwest Arabia may have taken its name from this person or persons. See J.A. Thompson, "Sheba," in *The Zondervan Pictorial Encyclopedia of the Bible*, ed. Merrill C. Tenney (Grand Rapids: Zondervan, 1976), 379.

2 Gus W. van Beek, "The Land of Sheba," in *Solomon and Sheba*, ed. James B. Pritchard (London: Phaidon, 1974), 40.

3 John J. Davis, "The Camel in Biblical Narratives," in *A Tribute to Gleason Archer*, ed. Walter C. Kaiser and Ronald F. Youngblood (Chicago: Moody, 1986), 141.

4 Patricia Crone, *Meccan Trade and the Rise of Islam* (Princeton, N.J.: Princeton Univ Press, 1987), 14.

5 While most do not argue with the queen's Arabic roots, some see her as the mother of the Ethiopian royal dynasty. Ethiopian people have a tradition that King Solomon married the Queen of Sheba and that they had a son, Menelik I. He lived in the palace in Jerusalem and became a believer in Yahweh. Menelik eventually returned to Ethiopia with other Hebrews and established the royal house of Ethiopia. See Graham Hancock, *The Sign and the Seal* (New York: Simon & Schuster, 1992), 103-04; Grant R. Jeffrey, *Armageddon, Appointment with Destiny* (New York: Bantam, 1992), 113-116; Edward Ullendorff, *Ethiopia and the Bible* (London: Oxford, 1968).

6 James B. Pritchard, "The Age of Solomon," in *Solomon and Sheba*, ed. James B. Pritchard (London: Phaidon, 1974), 19.

7 1 Kings 4:32.

8 1 Kings 10:1.

9 See Judges 14:12, the book of Proverbs, and Pritchard, 9.

10 Karl Chr.W.F. Bähr, "1 Kings," in *Commentary on the Holy Scriptures*, ed. John Peter Lange (Grand Rapids: Zondervan, 1872, 1960), 117.

11 Derek Kidner, *Proverbs* (Downers Grove, Ill: Inter-Varsity, 1964), 17.

12 Ibid., 16-17. See 1 Kings 4:30; Isaiah 19:11-12; 47:10; Jeremiah 49:7, Ezekiel 28:3; Daniel 1:4, 20; Obadiah 8; Zechariah 9:2; Acts 7:22.

13 1 Kings 4:31.

14 van Beek, 60-61.

15 Though it might be unusual in some ancient Near Eastern societies for a woman to be a leader and well-educated, Assyrian records do attest to queens in northern Arabia. See Crone, 14.

16 Lou H. Silberman, "The Queen of Sheba in Judaic Tradition,: 65-84; W. Montgomery Watt, "The Queen of Sheba in Islamic Tradition," 85-103; Edwin Ullendorff, "The Queen of Sheba in Islamic Tradition,"104-114; Paul F. Watson, "The Queen of Sheba in Christian Tradition," 115-151, in *Solomon and Sheba*, ed. James B. Pritchard (London: Phaidon, 1974).

17 From the *Midrash Mishle*, the midrash to the Book of Proverbs. See Silberman, 74.

18 Genesis 19:30-38. See Silberman, 75. Some have questioned this riddle not just because it is from Jewish tradition, but also because they wonder how the Queen of Sheba could have known about Lot. Muslims and Jews both see Abraham as their father, and even though the Queen of Sheba lived 1500 years before the founding of Islam, there may already have been a strong Abrahamic tradition. Those Arabs familiar with stories of Abraham may have also known those about his nephew, Lot. There also may have been Jews living at various oases in Arabia or Jewish traders who could have told the Old Testament stories.

19 1 Kings 4:34.

20 Donald J. Wiseman, *1 and 2 Kings* (Downers Grove, Ill.: Inter-Varsity, 1993), 129.

21 van Beek, "The Land of Sheba," 44.

22 Frankincense is a gum that exudes from trees or shrubs belonging to the genus *boswellia*. The finest quality of frankincense is obtained if incisions are made in the bark not too early in the year. This spice was used in the Temple and was an ingredient in holy oil. It is not native to Palestine. These trees still flourish on the desert plateau of Arabia, nourished by the tropical sun and the heavy dew, unique to that part of the world. The pungent and pleasurable smell emitted by burning frankin-

cense was and still is highly esteemed by the peoples of the Middle East. The heady and allusive scent of this precious perfume is highly valued. See *Flora and Fauna of the Bible*, 2nd ed. (London: United Bible Societies, 1980), 147-148.

Frankincense is associated with a sweet smell unto the Lord. God instructed Moses in the making of a sweet incense compound containing frankincense that was to be placed in the tabernacle of the congregation (Exodus 30:34-38). In the book of Revelation this sweet incense represents the prayers of the saints (Revelation 5:8).

23 Myrrh comes from the bush or tree *burseraceae* which is found in Arabia. It is a dark red gum with a strong aroma and a bitter taste. The finest of the myrrh exudes by itself without incision in the tree. It is a light-colored paste which soon hardens and becomes reddish-brown. Neither the myrrh tree or bush is native to Palestine which, of course, would increase its expense in that region. See *Flora and Fauna*, 121-122.

Myrrh was used in the preparation of anointing oil and in the manufacture of perfume. Wine mingled with myrrh was offered to Jesus on the cross as a pain-killing drug (Mark 15:23). It was also used along with aloes and other spices in the preparation of Jesus' body for burial.

24 van Beek, "The Land of Sheba," 46.

25 Esther 2:22. See van Beek, "The Land of Sheba," 45-47.

26 Crone, 17.

27 The Hebrew word for spices is not limited to condiments and is used for sweet-smelling aromas. In this case it probably included frankincense and myrrh.

28 1 Kings 10:10.

29 Crone, 93.

30 James B. Pritchard, "Introduction," in *Solomon and Sheba*, ed. James B. Pritchard (London: Phaidon, 1974), 9.

31 Crone, 21.

32 Carl Rasmussen, *Zondervan NIV Atlas of the Bible Tribute* (Grand Rapids: Zondervan, 1989), 27-28.

33 Crone, 19.

34 Wisemsn, 131. The servants mentioned in 1 Kings 10:5 may have been officials and officers of high rank.

35 van Beek, "The Land of Sheba," 63.

36 1 Kings 10:14-21.

37 1 Kings 12:4

38 1 Kings 4:22-23.

39 1 Kings 11:3.

40 Some believe the phrase "gave the queen of Sheba all she desired" (1 Kings 10:13) indicates a sexual relationship. Others think the queen is the bride in the Song of Solomon and the word *Shulamite* means simply "Solomon's girl" (Song 3:7; 6:13). Robert Davidson, *Ecclesiastes and The Song of Solomon* (Philadelphia: Westminster, 1986), 145. The Bible is not clear about either the sexual relationship or the marriage. We do know that the queen did not visit Solomon until at least the twenty-fourth year of his reign, but at the writing of the Song of Solomon the wives numbered sixty and the concubines eighty (Song 6:8). Considering that he had one-thousand female companions (1 Kings 11:3), this seems few indeed after twenty-four years.

41 Abraham Malamat, "A Political Look at the Kingdom of David and Solomon and Its Relations with Egypt," in *Studies in the Period of David and Solomon and Other Essays*, ed. Tomoo Ishida (Winona Lake, Ind: Eisenbrauns, 1982), 203-04.

[42] 1 Kings 6-7.

[43] 1 Chronicles 29:10-14.

[44] Crone, 170.

[45] F.E. Peters, *The Hajj* (Princeton, N.J.: Princeton Univ. Press, 1994), 20.

[46] van Beek, "The Land of Sheba," 61.

[47] Ibid., 61-62.

[48] Crone, 190-91.

[49] Peters, 41-45.

[50] Kidner, 17-18.

[51] 1 Kings 4:33.

[52] 1 Kings 3:9.

[53] Psalm 72.

[54] 2 Chronicles 5:18.

[55] A.A. MacRae, "Targum," in *The Zondervan Pictorial Encyclopedia of the Bible*, ed. Merrill C. Tenney (Grand Rapids: Zondervan, 1976), 597.

[56] See Psalms 8, 22, 34, 41, 69, 72.

[57] 2 Samuel 7:16.

[58] 2 Chronicles 9:6.

[59] 1 Kings 8:41-43.

[60] Philip K. Hitti, *History of the Arabs*, tenth edition, (New York: St. Martin's Press, 1970), 43.

[61] *The Jewish Encyclopedia*, vol.XI (New York: Funk & Wagnalls Co., 1905), 235.

[62] James I. Packer; Merrill C. Tenney; William White, Jr.; *The Bible Almanac* (Nashville: Thomas Nelson Publishers, 1980), 477.

[63] William Smith, *Dictionary of the Bible*, vol. IV, (Cambridge: Riverside Press, H.O. Houghton & Co., 1868-70), 3085-3086.

[64] R. Laird Harris; Gleason L. Archer, Jr.; Bruce K. Waltke; *Theological Wordbook of the Old Testament*, vol. I (Chicago: Moody Press, 1980), 27-28.

65 Grant R. Jeffrey, *Armageddon, Appointment with Destiny* (New York: Bantam Books, 1990), 113-115.

66 Smith, vol. IV, 2949.

67 Graham Hancock, *The Sign and the Seal,* (New York: Simon & Schuster, Inc., 1992), 103-104.

68 Jeffrey, 114-116.

69 It is interesting to note here that the Hebrew translation of the Aramaic Peshitta Text in Luke 24:27 uses the words *Moshe, Nebiim, Kethubim,* which mean "from Moses, the prophets and the writings." In Luke 24:44 the word Moses is amplified to "the Torah of Moses." The three words then, *Torah, Nebiim, Kethubim* are used in these two verses in describing Jesus' explanatory work about himself to his disciples. These words are simply "the Law, the Prophets, and the Writings," from which the Hebrew acronym Tanach is derived meaning the whole Hebrew scriptures. The formula "the Law and the Prophets" would be enough to include all the Hebrew canon. Therefore, the whole Hebrew canon speaks about Christ. *The New Covenant Aramaic Peshitta Text with Hebrew Translation,* edited by The Aramaic Scriptures Research Society in Israel (Jerusalem: The Bible Society, 1986), 116.

70 Hitti, 42.

71 Robert Davidson, *Ecclesiastes and The Song of Solomon* (Philadelphia: The Westminster Press, 1986), 145.

72 The Queen of Sheba gave Solomon gold, frankincense, and myrrh, which are the three gifts that the Magi brought to Jesus at his birth in order to worship Him. The early church father Tertullian (A.D. 160-230), as well as the Arabian historian Phillip Hitti, said that the Magi were Arabs. See Phillip K. Hitti, *The History of the Arabs* (New York: St. Martin's Press, 1970), 43.

73 Matthew 12:42.
74 Luke 11:31.
75 Isaiah 60:1-6; 19-20; Revelation 22:1-5.
76 John 8:56.
77 John 8:12.
78 Psalm 36:9.

Chapter Two

1 Paul P. Enns, *Ruth* (Grand Rapids: Zondervan, 1982), 28
2 Genesis 19:37.
3 Merrill C. Tenney, The Zondervan Pictorial Encyclopedia of the Bible, vol. 4 (Grand Rapids: Zondervan, 1976), 262.
4 Numbers 22-24.
5 Numbers 25.
6 Numbers 25:9.
7 Judges 3:14.
8 2 Kings 3:27.
9 Isaiah 15-16.
10 Jeremiah 48.
11 Ruth 1:22; 2:2, 6, 10, 21; 4:5, 10.
12 Enns, 13.
13 Isaiah 15.
14 Isaiah 16:5-6.
15 Herbert M. Wolf, *Interpreting Isaiah* (Grand Rapids: Zondervan, 1985), 118; cf. Isaiah 9:6; Amos 9:11.
16 Jeremiah 48:47.
17 Matthew 1:1.
18 Matthew 1:5.

19 Donald A. Carson, *Matthew*, in *The Expositor's Bible Commentary*, ed. Frank E. Gaebelein (Grand Rapids: Zondervan, 1984), 66.

20 Tenney, 347.

Chapter Three

1 "Mohammed's Night Journey to Heaven" at: http://www.prs.org/books book444.htm.

2 2 Kings 5:1-27.

3 Genesis 10:22.

4 Wayne T. Pitard, "Arameans," in Peoples of the Old Testament, eds. Alfred J. Hoerth, Gerald L. Mattingly, and Edw*in M. Yamauchi (Grand Rapids*: Baker, 1994), 207-230.

5 Genesis 22:21.

6 Genesis 25:20; 31:20.

7 Deuteronomy 26:5.

8 J.D. Douglas, *New Bible Dictionary* (Grand Rapids: Eerdmans, 1962), 55.

9 Pitard, 208.

10 Douglas, 56.

11 Pitard, 209.

12 Douglas, 59.

13 Donald J. Wiseman, *First and Second Kings* (Downers Grove, Ill: Inter-Varsity, 1993), 207.

14 Russell H. Dilday, *First and Second Kings* (Waco, TX: Word, 1987), 305.

15 Wiseman, 207.

16 2 Kings 5:18.

17 Richard Nelson, *First and Second Kings* (Louisville: John Knox, 1987), 183.

[18] Paul R. House, *First and Second Kings* (Nashville: Broadman, 1995) 273.

[19] Amos 9:7.

[20] Thomas E. McComiskey, "Amos," in *The Expositor's Bible Commentary*, ed. Frank E. Gaebelien (Grand Rapids: Zondervan, 1985), 327. Text of footnote.

[21] Matthew 4:13-16.

[22] Matthew 4:24; The Roman province of Syria included both Palestine and the ancient land of the Arameans.

[23] Luke 4:18-19.

[24] Luke 4:27.

[25] Acts 9:4-5.

[26] Acts 11:20-26.

[27] Acts 13:47.

Chapter Four

[1] Deuteronomy 7:1-5.

[2] Genesis 10:6; 15-20.

[3] There is no basis for the curse being the slavery of black-skinned peoples.

[4] Arthur C. Custance, Noah's Three Sons (Grand Rapids: Zondervan, 1975), 150.

[5] Some take *"servant of servants"* in a positive sense and purport that the descendants of Canaan through their technological abilities served mankind. It is true that the descendants of Canaan were highly skilled, but a curse is normally thought of as negative.

[6] Joshua 9:21-23.

[7] Genesis 9:25-27.

[8] Perhaps God extended the blessing to the descendants of Japheth, because he knew that the Jews would reject

the Messiah, and the responsibility of spreading the gospel of Christ would be given to the Gentiles (John 1:11-13; cf. Matthew 21:43). In that sense, Japheth was a prototype of the Gentile world.

9 Genesis 9:19.

10 Acts 8:26-39.

11 Acts 9:1-19.

12 Acts 10.

13 John Gray, *The Canaanites* (London: Thames & Hudson, 1964), 25; Donald Harden, *The Phoenicians* (New York: Praeger, 1962), 21.

14 Genesis 10:18.

15 Genesis 12:5; 15:16.

16 Numbers 13:29; Keith N. Schoville, "Canaanites and Amorites," in *Peoples of the Old Testament World*, eds. A.J. Hoerth, G.L. Mattingly, and E.M. Yamauchi (Grand Rapids: Baker, 1994), 166.

17 H. Jamieson, "Jericho," in *Zondervan Pictorial Encyclodedia of the Bible*, vol. 3, ed. Merrill C. Tenney (Grand Rapids: Zondervan, 1976), 451.

18 Joshua 2:1.

19 Joshua 2:10.

20 Joshua 2:10.

21 Joshua 2:11.

22 Joshua 3:15.

23 Schoville, 177-179.

24 Joshua 2:2.

25 Hebrews 11:31.

26 Hebrews 11:31.

27 Deuteronomy 9:4; 12:31.

28 Joshua 6:25.

29 Matthew 1:5.

30 Matthew 1:1-16.

31 Genesis 17:20; 25:1-2.
32 Genesis 17:9.
33 1 Kings 4:21.
34 Micah 5:2; Matthew 27:33.
35 Zechariah 14:2, 11; Matthew 24:21; Revelation 20:4.
36 Genesis 3:17.
37 2 Peter 3:10.
38 Revelation 21:2.
39 Genesis 3:17.
40 Galatians 3:26-29; cf. Genesis 12:3; Romans 4:11.

Chapter Five

1 Web:http//www.aims.org/AIMS/th 10-40 Window Project/Window Watchman/page 185.html.
2 Ibid.
3 Ibid.
4 Genesis 10:8-12.
5 Genesis 10:22.
6 H.W.F. Saggs, The Might that Was Assyria (London: Sigwick & Jackson, 1984), 2-22.
7 Georges Roux, Ancient Iraq (New York: Penguin, 1992), 148.
8 2 Kings 15:19-20.
9 2 Kings 15:29.
10 2 Kings 16:7-10.
11 2 Kings 17:3-6.
12 2 Kings 18:9-20:6.
13 Isaiah 7:17; Jeremiah 50:17; Ezekiel 32:22-23; Hosea 10:6; Nahum 1:11.
14 Arnold C. Brackman, *The Luck of Nineveh* (New York: McGraw-Hill, 1978), 3.
15 Ibid.

16 Ibid., 5.
17 Saggs, 201.
18 Ibid., 204.
19 Ibid., 206.
20 Genesis 28:14.
21 James Limburg, *Jonah* (Louisville Ky: Westminster/John Knox, 1993), 115-116.
22 Sura 10:98.
23 John Walton, *Jonah* (Grand Rapids: Zondervan, 1982), 36.
24 Jonah 3:4.
25 Gleason L. Archer, Jr., *A Survey of Old Testament Introduction* (Chicago: Moody, 1964), 300.
26 Some ancient cultures included animals in mourning ceremonies. See Leslie C. Allen, *Joel, Obadiah, Jonah and Micah* (Grand Rapids: Eerdmans, 1976), 224.
27 Jonah 3:8.
28 Jonah 3:9.
29 Jonah 4:1-11.
30 Allen, 234.
31 Allen, 235.
32 Terence E. Fretheim, *The Message of Jonah* (Minneapolis: Augsburg, 1977), 25; cf. Isaiah 56:6-8.
33 Matthew 12:40-41; 16:4; Luke 11:29.
34 Acts 2:31.
35 Acts 2:9.
36 Isaiah 9:7.
37 Isaiah 9:16.
38 Isaiah 20:6.
39 Isaiah 14:25.
40 Isaiah 19:24-25.
41 Isaiah 19:23.

Chapter Six

1. Idries Shah, *Tales of the Dervishes* (New York: Penguin, 1967), 63-65
2. Genesis 10:22.
3. Genesis 14.
4. John W. Limbert, Iran: At War with History (Boulder: Westview, 1987), 53.
5. For other verses about Elam, see Ezra 4:9-10; Isaiah 11:11; 21:2, 9; 22:6; Jeremiah 25:25; 49:35; Ezekiel 32:16,24
6. Genesis 10:2; see 2 Kings 17:6; *Isaiah 13:17; Jeremiah 25*:25; 51:11, 28; Danstview, 1987), 53.
7. M. Yamauchi, Persia and the Bible (Grand Rapids: Baker, 1990), 33.
8. Limbert, 29.
9. Ezra 1:1-2.
10. Jeremiah 29:10.
11. 2 Chronicles 36:22..
12. Isaiah 44-45.
13. Isaiah 44:2.
14. Isaiah 44:6.
15. Isaiah 44:6.
16. Genesis 12:3.
17. Isaiah 44:28.
18. Isaiah 45:1.
19. Isaiah 45:22.
20. Yamauchi, 92.
21. Limbert, 55.
22. Daniel 5:31.
23. Yamauchi, 59.

[24] Gleason L. Archer, Jr., *Daniel in Expositor's Bible Commentary*, ed. Frank E. Gaebelein (Grand Rapids: Zondervan, 1985), 76.

[25] Daniel 6:1.

[26] Daniel 6:2.

[27] Daniel 6:3.

[28] Daniel 6:7-17.

[29] Archer, 83.

[30] Yamauchi, 86.

[31] Ezra 5:17.

[32] Ezra 6:2.

[33] Ezra 6:3-12.

[34] Esther 4:14; see Gleason L. Archer, Jr., *A Survey of Old Testament Introduction* (Chicago: Moody, 1964), 403.

[35] Acts 2:17.

[36] Acts 2:36-38.

[37] Acts 2:39.

[38] Yamauchi, 396.

[39] Yamauchi, 417-418.

[40] Yamauchi, 443.

[41] Psalm 24:10.